Call to Joy

To order additional copies of *Call to Joy*, by Don Jacobsen, call 1-800-765-6955.

Visit us at www.reviewandherald.com for information on other Review and Herald products.

Christ's Radical Charter for a New Way to Live

Call to Joy

Don Jacobsen

IR

REVIEW AND HERALD® PUBLISHING ASSOCIATION
HAGERSTOWN, MD 21740

Texts credited to NIV are from the *Holy Bible, New International Version.* Copyright © 1973, 1978, 1984, International Bible Society. Used by permission of Zondervan Bible Publishers.

Bible texts credited to NRSV are from the New Revised Standard Version of the Bible, copyright © 1989 by the Division of Christian Education of the National Council of the Churches of Christ in the U.S.A. Used by permission.

Bible texts credited to RSV are from the Revised Standard Version of the Bible, copyright © 1946, 1952, 1971, by the Division of Christian Education of the National Council of the Churches of Christ in the U.S.A. Used by permission.

This book was
Edited by Jocelyn Fay
Copyedited by James Cavil
Cover designed by Emily Harding
Cover photo by FPG International Corp.
Interior designed by Toya Koch
Typeset: 11/14 Usherwood Book

PRINTED IN U.S.A.

05 04 03 02 01   5 4 3 2 1

R&H Cataloging Service
Jacobsen, Don, 1933-
    Call to joy: Christ's radical charter for a new way to live.

    Beatitudes. I. Title
                    226.93

ISBN 0-8280-1624-0

Dedication

To my wife, Ruthie, my inspiration

Acknowledgments

The material in this book first saw light as a series of sermons. It would never have made it into book form without the encouragement of Ray Tetz, president of Mind Over Media and a dear friend.

I am deeply grateful to some first-rate editors: Dan Day, Rosy Tetz, Jeannette Johnson, and Jocelyn Fay, and to all the folks I work with at Adventist World Radio who push me to excel.

Contents

1 | Jesus' Call to a New Life

"Let the word go forth from this time and place, to friend and foe alike, that the torch has been passed to a new generation of Americans—born in this century, tempered by war, disciplined by a hard and bitter peace, proud of our ancient heritage. . . . The energy, the faith, the devotion which we bring will light our country and all who serve it—and the glow from that fire can truly light the world.

"And so, my fellow Americans, ask not what your country can do for you. Ask what you can do for your country."

$\mathcal{M}$any Americans remember these words from John F. Kennedy's inaugural address as a powerful beginning to something new and exciting—a breaking-off point to a new start for the American spirit. That new start would include putting a person on the moon, driving off the nuclear missiles the U.S.S.R. was setting up in Cuba, and launching what has been termed "Camelot."

But even if you're not old enough to have heard these words "live," you're probably familiar with that final thought:

"Ask not what your country can do for you. Ask what you can do for your country." Nearly everyone who heard those words was stirred by this new way of thinking about patriotism, uttered as it was in a time when cynicism threatened to undermine how Americans saw themselves. Something in us responds to that challenge and causes us to say, "Yes, that's how I want to be. I want to have a part in changing my world."

It's interesting how much the inaugural speeches of our leaders tell us about their character and the direction they intend to lead. That was certainly true with JFK's inaugural. It is also true about the inaugural speech that Jesus made many years earlier—the speech we call the Sermon on the Mount.

Some time ago I became very interested in the Sermon on the Mount, especially the Beatitudes section. I began to study it intensely, to try to understand it better. Why would Jesus choose this particular message for launching His mission to Planet Earth? What was He wanting to say to us in our generation? I spent about six months, just about every day, in the Beatitudes. All this time I was praying for God's understanding, and I studied with a Bible dictionary beside me, along with commentaries and word studies and other books. I was trying to understand what Jesus was saying in that set of Beatitudes—what He had for me to learn as a growing Christian.

I wasn't preparing for a sermon or a book during this process. I just wanted to hear what the Lord was saying to me, even as He spoke to His disciples so long ago in His inaugural address. What I found was a profound passage of Scripture. I found some things I'd never noticed before about what it means to be a Christian. I found new excitement for my own Christian pilgrimage, and a new appreciation of the radical nature of the kingdom Jesus came to establish.

I found a new understanding of Him, too, because His character is revealed in this inaugural speech. He is pure. He is meek. He is holy. I want to be like that. In spite of all the stress and pressure, all the aggravation and conflict in which He was embroiled throughout His lifetime, Jesus possessed the deep joy, the tranquillity, and the peace I want in my life.

Don't you want that in your life? The desire for it is one of the reasons this message is so relevant today. We all need what Jesus displayed.

This inaugural message by Jesus became very important to me again, not too long ago, when I was asked to assume the leadership of Adventist World Radio, with its far-reaching ministry to men and women in parts of the world that are very difficult to reach in any other way except by radio. I realized at that point in my life I was being asked to serve in a new way, as the leader of a ministry with awesome potential for sharing the gospel to the world. I was humbled by the trust God and my church were placing in me, and nearly overwhelmed by my own inadequacy for providing the kind of leadership the task deserved.

I knew I needed a word from God as I stepped forth in faith. So I turned again to this transforming message of hope that I've entitled *Call to Joy*.

I also believe the church today needs a transforming message of hope. And so I present to you my understanding of what Jesus had to say. In this book we're going to look together at this momentous passage of Scripture, this invitation to happiness, this radical charter for a new way to live, this inaugural address: the Beatitudes.

I'd like you to think about what follows in several ways. First, I hope that this book becomes a help to you in your own devotional journey. Jesus spoke these words to His disciples and to the others in the crowd in order to signal a radical departure, a call to change the way they saw their world. And He meant it for each of them, personally.

Keep that in mind as you read these pages. None of us can read what Jesus said that day without being changed.

I've organized the book in such a way that you can use it as a part of your small group discussion activity in your church, if you so choose. To help facilitate this, I've added questions at the end of each chapter to make it easier for a group leader to initiate a discussion, to focus the group on themes that lend themselves to redemptive conversation.

And I've provided a prayer ideas section—themes that suggest topics about which you can pray or directions you or your group might want to move in light of what the chapter discussed.

The Call to Change

This first chapter is about setting the stage. Before we launch into a study of this inaugural address by Jesus, let's take a look at what had been going on during His life and ministry at the moment He spoke these words. How was the scene set when Jesus gave this tremendous pronouncement? What were the members of the audience thinking about? What had Jesus just been through in His own journey?

In Matthew 4 we find that Jesus has just been baptized in the Jordan River by that remarkable prophetic figure whom we call John the Baptist. The entire experience was shaped by the miraculous. First the heavens had opened, and for one of the few times in history, the very voice of God had been heard. Then immediately Jesus entered into the wilderness to experience an almost overpowering series of temptations. You can be sure that Satan was there in person. He did not send an understudy to the wilderness to try to lead Jesus astray. Here was his big chance to try to lead into sin in some way—even by a thought—the Son of God.

But Satan failed. Jesus chose to trust God and was successful in overcoming the worst that the enemy could deliver. It was a pivotal moment in the redemption saga!

Then the scene changes again. Jesus returns to the busy world where His ministry would take place. Matthew 4:17 says, "From that time Jesus began to preach, saying, 'Repent, for the kingdom of heaven is at hand'" (RSV).

Here is Jesus' call to radical change. That's what the word "repent" means: change. Jesus was not preaching about business as usual. He was calling the world to something dramatically different—to repent and embrace change.

His was not a call to compromise. It was not a call to concession. It was not a call to conformity. It was a call to change. And we in the Christian church must never forget that. Jesus picks us up anywhere He finds us. He loves us, even when others might find us unlovable. But He'll never be content to leave us there. He wants far more for us than that! He wants us to become something changed, something new, something enlivened by His power.

But the word "change" is one of those words that carries frightening connotations. Change is not always a comfortable word—mostly because it infers that we are to become "different." And the thought of becoming different often makes us cringe—especially when we're expected to be different from the crowd.

Being different has a positive side, too. During its dramatic start-up years, Apple Computer ran a series of ads in magazines and on television that were simple yet powerful. Each had just one face, the face of a distinguished figure who had made a difference in the world—Mother Teresa, Mahatma Gandhi, Martin Luther King, Jr., and others. The caption said simply, "Think Different."

It made all the English teachers cringe, but what a powerful image! Think different and change the world! You and I know that the ads would have been even more profound if they had shown the face of Jesus. God wants us to "think different" and change the world.

But it's not easy to become agents of change.

Have you noticed the chameleon-like tendency that lies not far under the skin of all of us? There is comfort in being one of the crowd. When we're with a noisy group from the office and everyone is roasting the boss, it's easy to slip into that same frame of mind. Or when we're with a pious group discussing last-day events, it's so easy to feel pious. It's easy to fit into the climate in which we find ourselves.

But not to be willing to be different is not to be Christian.

As Jesus embarks upon His ministry, He says, "Repent. Change. You are not by nature what you ought to be. I want you to be different from what's going on in the world around you." We ought to make no apologies for being different from the crowd. If we are willing to say "I don't mind being different if I'm being different for the right reason," it can have a dramatic effect on how we feel about ourselves and on the influence we can have on others. We can then see the contrast of the way we think and act as being a powerful witness—a statement of our allegiance to Jesus, who stood in stark contrast with His world.

You have probably felt as I have when I've allowed myself to be drawn into a discussion I knew I shouldn't join: discouraged and ashamed. You feel like Adam and Eve in the garden after they'd sinned—hiding in the bushes, realizing they'd let God down, and not knowing what to do about it. But we can't really hide from God—or from the consequences of letting ourselves slip into these common situations in which we're compromised.

On the other hand, to be willing to say "This is wrong and I will not do it" gives us reason to stand a little taller. To stand for the right when champions are few is an act of heaven-ordained courage. It can give new meaning and new excitement to our lives. It transforms us. In a very real sense it is a gesture of Christlikeness.

To become like Christ is to become increasingly unlike everyone who is not a Christian. That's important because of what happens if we forget it. Sometimes Christians reason, "Shouldn't we be as much like those around us as we can—so long as there is no moral compromise—so they don't feel uncomfortable when they are with us?"

That sounds reasonable. But is it *right?* A good example of the flaw in that logic has been the development in the Christian church of gospel rock music. Some reasoned, "Let's take the medium of rock music and put Christian words with it. They'll like our music, and then they'll listen to our words."

But it is my observation that gospel rock seldom produces those results. It is a flawed vehicle for communicating the exalted themes of God—typically drowning out with its strong beat the very Christian message it proposes to share. It represents a kind of compromise to the popular culture, and the Christian church never succeeds by compromise. Music is such a universal language that a Spirit-led church can write and perform that which has appeal across all cultures.

Similarly, there is another area of popular religious culture that has flawed logic. Some churches have been willing to ordain homosexual pastors to the ministry. They do so as a gesture of welcome to all, so those with "alternative lifestyles" will not feel excluded from the Christian community. However, in so doing, these churches give up a measure of their power to draw a clear line between God's mercy and forgiveness and His clear call to a life consistent with the highest moral principles. It is wonderful to be inclusive. But we must also be consistent with the character of Jesus.

Another aspect of Jesus' call to change is the way we relate to it, as individuals, with our predisposition to sin. I have discovered that the thing I do by nature is quite often wrong. In other words, when I'm faced with a decision, unless I stop and intentionally submit that decision to the lordship of Jesus Christ, as often as not I do the wrong thing. Whether it's the way I respond to my wife, or to a letter that comes, or to a cantankerous neighbor, or to the car ahead of me in traffic—my natural response is usually the wrong one. And that's exactly what Jesus is getting at here when He says, "Repent. Change. I want you to move away from what you are by nature to what I am by nature."

But didn't the apostle Paul say something about fulfilling the gospel commission to be all things to all people? Didn't Paul talk about adapting to the people around him, so that he could win them to Christ? (See 1 Corinthians 9:19-23.) Yes, Paul did say that. He did it himself, with redemptive effect. But he was pleading with the church to try to *understand* worldly culture, to use it as a powerful tool in reaching people. He wasn't calling on us to *embrace* that worldly culture. He was asking the church to *build bridges of caring and understanding,* not compromise.

Recently I was visiting the AWR studio in Hong Kong, and they told me this story. If you have visited Hong Kong, or even seen pictures, you know that it is a city of high-rise housing. It is as though someone planted high-rise seeds that grew into a bumper crop. Thousands of families live in a square mile, 20, 30, 40 stories above the ground.

As in many of the world's great cities, with so many people in such a tight space, recreation areas for the young people are at a premium. There are what they call "social rooms" in most of the buildings. Unfortunately, what happens in these "social rooms" is seldom supervised and not always positive. The music is generally raucous, and drugs are common. Some people wanted the government to provide condoms; others wanted the rooms shut down altogether.

Some of our church folks, though—concerned about the future of the children in these artificial neighborhoods— got permission from the government to use some of these "social rooms" for a different purpose. After school and on weekends they began holding classes. They provided tutoring services and health classes. Sometimes they played games. Sometimes the activity involved just listening to the kids read. Sometimes they met with a group; sometimes one-on-one. Some of those helping were professional teachers; some were just plain folks. On the weekends they provided character-development lessons using the Bible as their textbook. The point is, without compromise, they met the kids on their own turf and turned an unfortunate circumstance into a life-changing environment.

Christ's call to His church—then and today—is a call to change . . . change that cuts into the dull, mundane, destructive pattern of our secular culture and presents a new, far better, more joyous way of living. And we ought not to be surprised if we're out of step with the rest of the world when we introduce this sort of change. Our assignment is to bring redemptive change that calls us from what we are by nature to become like Him.

How Change Happens

But how does that change take place?

In the Beatitudes, Jesus paints a picture of what a transformed believer would look like. "Take a look at this," He says. "Here is what you can become." But when we look at that noble picture we don't see ourselves. You and I were not born with any of the traits on that list.

So how do we get them? It is important to keep in sharp focus how these traits become reality in our lives. They are not behaviors we try to paint on the outside. We do not look through the list in Matthew 5 and say "H'mmm. Blessed are the meek. OK, from now on I'm going to be more meek. Meekness. Meekness. This is Monday, and I've got to remember to be meek today."

That's a dead-end street: either we accomplish it and become proud of our spiritual accomplishments or we fail and get discouraged.

The reality is quite different. Those are traits Jesus brings with Him when He comes into our lives. We don't seek the trait; we seek Him. And when He comes in, when He takes possession of us, He brings those traits with him.

This is a new idea to a lot of people, I know—even to a lot of Christians. Some of us never get it right. Yet it is absolutely foundational to an understanding of what it means to be a Christian. I was visiting with a man over our backyard fence in Riverside, California, one day, when he explained to me why he couldn't be a Christian. "There are just too many rules for me to keep," he said. "There are too many things I like to do that I'd have to give up." Many people see the Christian life in that way—a long list of rules and prohibitions and things we have to sacrifice to the cause if we want to join up. The fact is, of course, that the Christian life is nothing like that at all. It's not a matter of what we give up. It's a matter of what we get. And as for the changes on display, they're what He does in us. When we invite Him to be Lord of all, He comes to live within and He changes us. We become like Him by inviting Him to take up residence.

We do not become humble or pure or meek by deciding we are going to be humble or pure or meek, but by deciding we are going to be His. He brings with Him those traits of humbleness and purity and meekness. The more like Him we become, the more like them we become. And the more access we give Him to our lives, the more those traits begin to surface.

In other words, in the Sermon on the Mount, Jesus is not saying, "Here's a list of things for you to measure up to. I want you to start acting like this and stop doing that." Instead He's saying, "I want you to become adopted members of My kingdom, and when that happens, this is what you're going to look like—because you will develop a family likeness." Cause and effect. If we connect with Christ, we're going to be changed. There is no shortcut. There is no way we can work up enough willpower to transform ourselves. It's all a result of entering into a redemptive relationship with Jesus.

So rather than being a discouraging prospect, there is good news here when we talk about change. When we read that list we don't need to say, "I can never achieve that. I can never do that on my own." He has never asked us to. Rather, He has said, "Spend some time with Me. Let My Word wash in." He says, "Let the telescope of My Word look deeply into your heart. Let Me have access to your motives. Submit your decisions to My lordship in your life every day. And as you do that, you'll start to look like this."

Now, that's good news, because it's not something we

have to achieve. It is simply something we have to remember to keep accepting. That's righteousness by faith. It is not a checklist that we go through to see how well we're doing. It's a relationship we enter into, and as we spend time with Him, as He becomes, increasingly, Lord of our lives, He implants deeply within us that which He *is* by nature. Now, there's a great transaction if I ever saw one!

The Transforming Impact of Christian Community

But there is another part of this picture that is equally important. This transformation isn't just something that happens to us in isolation. It happens as we become part of a Christian community. This may be a new thought for some. But it becomes increasingly clear as we move through the preamble to this mountaintop sermon.

"As he walked by the Sea of Galilee, he saw two brothers, Simon, who is called Peter and Andrew his brother, casting a net into the sea; for they were fishermen. And he said to them, 'Follow me, and I will make you fishers of men.' Immediately they left their nets and followed him" (Matt. 4:18-20, RSV).

I like that. At this point in the development of His kingdom, Jesus begins to build a community. He begins to bring people together to be with Him. A solo Christian is an anomaly. It's like trying to have a university with one student or an army with one soldier.

When Phil Follett and I visited more than a hundred AWR listeners in central China, we learned a great deal about how the need for community is born in the heart as soon as a love for Jesus takes root there. In city after city new Christians we met told us how they had accepted Jesus after listening to the radio—and how their conversion immediately triggered a search for others who shared the same beliefs. Clearly God has called Christian believers together to be members in a community. Much of what needs to happen in our lives cannot happen unless we are bona fide parts of that community. That explains why the simile of the family is used so often in Scripture to describe believers who are knit together by the common bond of the fatherhood of God.

God made us social creatures who need to be nurtured and to give nurture.

It is a deeply important spiritual dynamic. What needs to happen to us spiritually happens only partially when we're on our knees or alone before the open Word. The rest of it must happen as we draw strength from the Christian community, interacting with our brothers and sisters and being used by God in their lives also.

Why is this so? It's because God made us this way. He made us to need one another. You are very important to me. We need each other. Jesus began to draw people together so they could function together, so they could be active together, so they could worship together. That's part of the package of being a Christian. To stand on the periphery of the church and touch it only infrequently or from a distance is to limp as a Christian—and who wants to be a limp Christian?

There is another compelling reason for community. Together we can be much more effective for the kingdom than any of us can be alone. You touch lives I never touch. You know people I've never met. God needs you to reach them because He knows I can't.

For example, I might wish I had an attractive, well-written magazine I could give to my friends that would help lead them to Christ. But it would be prohibitively expensive for me to write and print such a magazine with only enough copies for me to give to those I meet. But as a church community we have a deep pool of talented writers and artists and printers. As they join together in the project, and as others of my brothers and sisters decide they can use the same missionary journal—voilà! *Signs of the Times* is born. Why? Because of the rich resources of the Christian community.

On the eastern tip of central Africa is the country of Somalia, with a population of 7 million. I want to tell them about the love of Jesus, but I don't speak Somali. Neither am I a radio engineer. Providentially, God leads us to a young Somali living outside of his country who agrees to produce programs for his compatriots. We begin to broadcast, and within days letters come from listeners telling us they are hearing our broadcasts and have accepted Jesus as their Saviour. I am not an engineer, and I do not speak Somali. But through the community, God makes the impossible possible. I can be part of that, helping to make it all happen, and so can you!

Jesus called His disciples that they might be with Him. And in being with Him, they were with each other. There was something powerful going on between Jesus and the entire group that followed Him. On the mountainside that beautiful afternoon they shared an event in community, an event so powerful that it stays in our minds even today.

How important is your church to you? How important is the fellowship you know there? What happens in the foyer after church? What happens around the dinner table after church? How recently have you phoned someone to say "I just wanted you to know I prayed for you this morning"? Maybe that would be a good assignment this week.

Jesus called the Christian community to be together because things happen to us, and through us, when we come together in His name. Together, by His grace, we're able to accomplish things we could never do alone.

The Healing Presence of Jesus

There is something about being with Jesus that is absolutely transforming. A healing presence. Consider this startling statement:

"And he went about all Galilee, teaching in their synagogues and preaching the gospel of the kingdom and healing every disease and every infirmity among the people" (Matt. 4:23, RSV).

Did you know there were entire villages in which—after Jesus passed through—not one sick person was left behind? The main reason Jesus did that was because He loved the people who lived there, and He hated to see them sick. Our Lord is like that. He cares about people as individuals. He is touched by our pain. He is moved with compassion. Wouldn't it have been exciting to follow along behind Him as He went from one village to another?

Have you ever, in your imagination, recreated one of these Bible scenes?

Walk along beside Jesus as He approaches a man and touches his eyes. Suddenly, for the first time, the man can see! What kind of emotions do you suppose raced through the heart of that man who had never seen before, never seen his wife's face, never seen his little boy's smile?

What an experience it would have been to walk along beside Jesus and see Him approach that leper, the man who had become a social outcast, away from his family and friends, away from his job and home, away from his life in a living death. Imagine being able to see Jesus touch that man and then to watch the expression on the leper's face as he began to grasp that now his fingers were restored and his feet were whole again and he was not unclean—he could go home!

When Jesus said, "Go and show yourself to the priests," the man went to the synagogue and walked intently into that little room. Imagine the expression on his face as he walked up to the priest and said, "Look at me. I'm healed. I'm whole. I'm no longer a leper." Now walk beside him after he's pronounced clean. Keep up with him, if you can, as he makes his way back to his house, to the wife he thought he would never see again. Look at the wonder on her face as he walks into the house and they embrace.

Now step back and consider this: He wants to do that to a whole planetful of people, you and me included. What a wonderful God!

Happiness Is

We've seen something of the preamble to the Sermon on the Mount—the setting out of which it grew. Now Jesus withdraws to the mountain. Now the crowds begin to gather about Him, and He sits down and describes to them the wonderful changes they can expect to see taking place in their lives.

Already in the story a few men have broken with their family and friends and jobs to organize themselves around Jesus. These "disciples" come to Him, a bit like guerrilla troops coming to their leader, staking their lives on Him. There's a great deal they don't know yet. He must show them the way, the strategy by which this mission is going to succeed. But I find it interesting that Jesus does not talk to them now about strategy; He talks to them about becoming.

It surely is no accident that before He talks about going or preaching or proclaiming or witnessing He says, "First of all, this is what you need to be. This is the kind of change that needs to take place."

And so He begins:

"Seeing the crowds, he went up on the mountain, and when he sat down his disciples came to him. And he opened his mouth and taught them, saying: 'Blessed . . .'" (Matt. 5:1-3, RSV).

I want to spend a little time marching around the word "blessed," because it's the foundation for so much that follows. What does it mean? Of all the other words He might have chosen, why did He choose this one? Of this much we can be sure, it wasn't an accident.

I don't know what translation or paraphrase of the Scriptures you prefer in your personal study of the Bible. There are many, and each has its appeal. Different words are used for "blessed" in different translations. One of them is "happy." That's a good word, and I'll use it often. The only problem is that "happy" is a bit shallow and over-used; it doesn't go deep enough into the real meaning. Furthermore, it suggests happenstance. That is, it implies that how we feel is affected by what happens to us. And that is definitely not the meaning Jesus intended to convey.

Another word your version may use is "fortunate." I'm not sure that hits it either, because it seems to infer luck. One translation I read said "spiritually prosperous." I'm impressed with that, I guess, but I have to admit I'm not sure I really understand it. "To be envied," another translation says. I don't know if I like that, either.

"Full of deep joy" is the translation I like best, because it seems to fit most precisely the profound insight Jesus wants us to discover.

The point is, the idea behind "blessed" is bigger than any single English word can convey. But it's important to wrestle with it, because Jesus uses it as the keynote word in His inaugural address. In the initial utterance of this, the most famous sermon ever preached, Jesus addresses Himself to the supreme desire of every human heart: true joy.

Here's the reason this is such a radical charter for His new kingdom: While everyone seeks happiness, the majority seek for it in ways that can bring only sorrow.

Jesus says, "The desire for true happiness is a God-given desire. I want you to be happy. But let Me help you find it in a way that doesn't turn to ashes tomorrow."

I have a friend who does a lot of traveling. Some years ago he was often accosted in airports by those young people we call Moonies. If you ever meet one of these earnest young people, you never forget it. Just as you are rushing to your gate with two suitcases, a garment bag, and a briefcase, they want to stop you and try to convince you to join them.

Well, my friend developed a response that I thought was inspired. He carried a business card in his pocket, and when somebody accosted him like that, instead of being rude or just shrugging them off, he would reach into his pocket, pull out one of his cards, and say, "I don't have time to talk to you right now, but one of these days what you're into is going to become hollow and empty, and when it does, call me collect, any time, day or night." Then he'd hand them his card and hurry on.

I like that approach for several reasons, not the least of which is that it depicts the point Jesus is making. Anything other than a total, unreserved commitment to Him is going to be hollow tomorrow. Without Him to direct it, life is like that. But He can change it, and He wants to. In fact, He can do that for you right now. Maybe that unreserved commitment to Christ is not a reality for you at this point in your life. I want to invite you to leave that behind and accept this commitment.

Perhaps it's a rather startling thought at this moment,

given all you're facing, but please read this carefully: *The most readily identifiable, outward characteristic of the Christian is joy.*

That is contrary to the way most people see the Christian church. Many think of Christians as severe, driven people, preoccupied with being good and getting saved. Yet Jesus says the most readily identifiable outward characteristic of the Christian is joy. If something has happened inside, it will show.

I was in a motel lobby in Seattle one evening, filling out the registration form. A friend of mine walked in, a man I hadn't seen for a long time. As he approached the desk the clerk said to him, "Good evening."

But my friend replied, "Good morning."

The clerk and I looked at each other and smiled rather indulgently. I think our eyes were exchanging the thought: *This guy's a smart aleck.*

But my friend seemed to read what we were thinking, and he said, "Hey, that's not just an empty phrase. I'm a Christian, and it's always morning in my heart." I was impressed enough that I remember the story even today.

Now, that may not be your thing. You may not feel comfortable sharing your faith in Christ in that way. That's fine. We're all different. But somewhere deep inside every Christian there lives that buoyancy that says, "It's always morning in my heart."

Did you ever meet Christians who looked as though they lived on a diet of dill pickles? It's a fairly easy habit to get into. When there's pressure, when there's stress, when there's deep grief, when things aren't going well financially, or at school, or in your marriage, or physically . . . when you've got your own custom-built set of difficulties, how can there be that buoyancy, that radiance, that deep inner joy that Jesus is talking about?

May I suggest the key? It depends on our value system.

Let me work on that a little more. If our lives are built around something that can be taken away from us, then there will be occasions of despair. But if our lives are built around that which cannot be taken away, there is always reason for a deep inner peace. Jesus has set up residence in our hearts, and the focus of our lives becomes that which can never be taken away.

We can lose some of the stuff on the periphery. We can lose some of the incidentals. We can even lose some precious treasures. But that which is most important can never be taken away, and that can provide us with a deep, abiding inner peace—which is what Jesus is talking about.

I'm sure you know the story of Joni Eareckson-Tada.* On a hot day in July 1967, she dived into shallow water in the Chesapeake Bay. Joni struck a submerged rock and broke her neck, instantly becoming paralyzed from the neck down. It was a miracle she didn't drown.

But the greater miracle is that the tragedy didn't break her spirit. To read Joni's book is to read the heroic saga of a young woman who has struggled with despair and discouragement. She lost the ability to do almost anything for herself except chew her food and talk. Here is the story of a young woman whose value system was built around something that could not be taken away from her. And even in the face of that tragedy she could surface with an abiding deep peace that has not only buoyed her own spirit, but has blessed millions through her testimony, her music, her daily radio program, and her painting.

"Filled with deep joy," Jesus would say, "are those who have found something so strong in life that it cannot be taken from them."

So here we are. The stage is set. We're all gathered around, waiting to hear what Jesus is about to say in this inaugural message. Our hearts are open. We're sitting on the edge of our seats, ready to be transformed by His words, ready to get our marching orders for becoming active in His service.

What is Jesus going to say?

LISTENING TO GOD: THOUGHT QUESTIONS

☞ How do I really feel about "being different" in a world that seems to value conformity? Does the idea make me uncomfortable?

☞ What if some of the significant others in my world don't understand why I'm beginning to make some of the changes in my life God seems to be asking me to make? What should I do? How should I relate to them? How should their views affect my decisions?

☞ How can I build bridges of caring, not compromise? Is it possible to be different from those around us without seeming to condemn them in a self-righteous manner?

☞ What if I find myself being drawn into the world I'm trying to reach for Christ? What is the first thing I should do? Is there a way that the Christian community can help?

☞ In what ways might I become a more active agent for change within the Christian community of which I am part? How do I start?

SHARING WITH GOD: THE MINISTRY OF PRAYER

Lord, not only am I without eloquence in prayer, but I often don't know the best things to ask for. Help me find the words.

"I know that You have drawn me into circumstances this

week that gave me opportunities to learn things You wanted me to know, as well as opportunities to be an agent for change in my world. And I know I haven't always heard what You were saying or acted as quickly or effectively as I might have. So I ask You to give me a heart more like Yours, so I can discern more quickly this week what You want me to see and do. And I ask You to give me a bold spirit, so I can respond to Your promptings and act for You decisively.

"Thank You for allowing me to be part of what You are doing in the world.

"Amen."

---

* Joni Eareckson, with Joe Musser, *Joni* (Grand Rapids, Mich.: Zondervan, 1976).

2. The Happy Poor

Blessed are the poor in spirit, for theirs is the kingdom of heaven (Matt. 5:3, RSV).

Strange statement, isn't it? Even today we grapple with the words. Who are the poor in spirit, and what does God see in them that they should be inheritors of the kingdom? What does it all mean, anyway?

Somehow the phrase "poor in spirit" leaves us confused and perhaps even disillusioned. I thought we were talking about being radiantly joyful.

If someone were to ask you to describe the members of your church, how would you describe them? Would you say "They're a bunch of 'poor-spirited' people"? And if you had to say that, would it strike you that people of that sort would be attractive to the world? Would they be the sort of people Jesus could use to win a broken world?

Yet that seems to be what Jesus is saying here. He is describing the citizens of His kingdom, and He says the number one characteristic is that they are poor in spirit. But given the context that this is part of Jesus' message about joy, we have to assume that these people are somehow filled with true joy. How is that possible? Apparently there is something in this statement that is not immediately obvious.

I'd like to explore three truths I see as inherent in this first of the Beatitudes, and I believe that as we understand them it will blossom like a rose.

Where Arrogance Comes From

The opposite of spiritual poverty is pride, and pride inclines us to think more highly of ourselves than we ought to.

But have you ever thought about why people act in a proud manner? What is it that gives birth to arrogance in the human heart? There is a great insight here in the statement Jesus makes.

One of the curses hanging over our world is that people and nations tend to think more highly of themselves than they ought to. Can you imagine what might happen at the United Nations if, with every opening session, all the delegates from all over the world came together and washed each other's feet? It would give a different flavor, I suspect, to that session of the United Nations and to whatever discussion might follow.

I remember visiting the demilitarized zone between North and South Korea. The two halves of that troubled land are technically still at war after more than a half century, so they have cut out of the jungle a little community with a few buildings where representatives of the north and the south come to sit around the "peace table" and talk about uniting North and South Korea. We call it Panmunjom.

The day we were there the guide told us about some of the ceremonies that go on. For instance, it's more honorable in that culture to be the last to arrive. Sometimes the meetings may be days late getting started because each side wants to be last to the table.

Then, once they get inside, the northern delegates sit along one side of the table and the southern delegates sit along the other. Each side has a flag in front of them on the table. However, it's more honorable to have your flag a little taller than that of the other side. So there is this ongoing battle to see who can get the biggest flag to stand on the table while they're negotiating.

I tell this story not to be critical but because it is such an enlightening commentary on human nature. It's the sort of thing that permeates our lives. When pride takes hold of us, we assume an exaggerated role in our family, in the neighborhood, in church, at work, at school, everywhere.

It's pride that makes us bristle when we're criticized. Pride makes us want to get even.

It's pride that makes it difficult for us to say to a spouse or child or parents, "I'm sorry; I was wrong. Those were unkind words; please forgive me." Or "What I did was certainly not a loving thing to do, and I apologize."

It's pride that demands that we come out on top in every disagreement. But logically, to win every argument is to have only losers for friends. It's pride that makes us feel threatened when someone disagrees with us. And it's pride that makes us try to find ways to pull them down so that we feel more right or somehow justified in our position.

It's pride that discourages us because we have not achieved in some area as brilliantly as we would have liked, or have not done what we think people expect us to accomplish. We don't look as good to ourselves or to others as we wish we did, and that's depressing and discouraging. Pride does that.

Remember our premise. If it's true that "happy are the poor in spirit," the reverse is also true: "unhappy are the arrogant." And all the things we do to support our pride end up turning on us and sucking away the happiness we desire.

Should I Admit, Then, That I'm a Jerk?

A second statement I'd like to make about this first beatitude is that it does not teach that we ought to run to and fro belittling ourselves. Jesus taught no such thing. There are people who have trouble accepting a compliment. If you say, "You have a lovely dress on tonight," a person with this frame of mind might say, "Well, I got it from a resale shop, and it's rather out of style." Or if you say, "I really appreciated your song this morning in church," he'll say, "Did you hear my voice crack?" Some people feel it is somehow very spiritual to belittle themselves.

But Jesus didn't teach that. During the time when He walked the paths of the Middle East there was a well-established pecking order. To the Greek, the only person who counted was the person who could think. To the Roman, the only person who was important was the person who could conquer. To the Jew, the only person who mattered was the person who kept the law. And then Jesus came and introduced a radical new way of looking at people. Suddenly everybody was important.

Here's why that's a valuable insight: When God's people understand their true worth, we don't need to try and pretend to be something we aren't. Instead, we can be like the little boy Ruth Murdoch told me about when she was a professor at Andrews University in Michigan:

A little boy about 5 years old was sitting on the front porch one day, looking across the street to where a neighbor was hanging up her wash. The wind was blowing, and she was having a difficult time hanging up some big pieces of laundry. It seemed that about the time she'd get one piece up, the previous one would get away.

Another woman walked down the sidewalk in front of the house where the little boy was sitting, and she stopped to talk to him. As they talked, they watched this neighbor together. Pretty soon the little boy said, "It's too bad she doesn't have a nice little boy like me to help her hang up her washing!"

When we begin to understand that we are valuable enough for Someone to want to die in our place, then there begins to dawn on us the understanding of our value, that we count, that we're important. There is nobody else like you in all this world. God made you, and you are so precious to Him that He has decided not to make another like you. A true understanding of our importance in the eyes of God takes away our need to be inappropriately proud of our accomplishments or destructively self-critical.

When you and I stand accused before the Judge of the universe and Satan presents the charges against us, he has an airtight case—and he doesn't even have to exaggerate. The verdict is just: We have forfeited the right to life. But then Jesus steps forward and says, "Wait! No! I'll take his place. I'll take her place." On the very center page of Ellen G. White's classic book on the life of Christ entitled *The Desire of Ages* is this incredible statement: "Jesus did not count heaven a place to be desired while we were lost" (p. 417). The more you ponder that sentence, the more overwhelming it becomes.

Antique dealers tell me that the worth of an object depends on the price someone is willing to pay for it. Now, there's a theological insight!

Have you ever met people who seem determined to impress everyone they meet, bragging about themselves and monopolizing the conversation? After listening to them for a while we go away thinking, *Wow, he's really vain,* or *She's really got a big head.* Do you know why people do that? It's because they feel inadequate and inferior. They say to themselves, "Here's one little piece of me that's OK. Here's one thing I can do. I'd like people to notice that; then maybe they won't notice all the places that I'm not OK."

But Jesus says that when we're His, we don't have to play that game. He can give us the security that enables us to say to ourselves, "I am of value. I don't have to run around trying to impress everybody. Neither do I have to tell them how terrible I am. I can be who He's making me to be. I can be who I am." And that permits us to smile, to laugh at our mistakes, to accept criticism and say, "Thank you. I'm glad you pointed that out. I really need to know that." Or to accept a compliment graciously and say, "Well, thank you. I'm glad." No wonder Jesus could say, "Happy are people like this."

Please notice this interesting statement about Jesus: "Now before the feast of the Passover, when Jesus knew that his hour had come to depart out of this world to the Father, having loved his own who were in the world, he loved them to the end" (John 13:1, RSV). It was the Last Supper, and Jesus was going to wash His disciples' feet. Verse 3 says that Jesus knew "that he had come from God and was going to God" (RSV). He knew who He was and He knew whose He was. He knew that He was loved by the Father. He knew that His place in the Father's heart was unconditional. And He could be secure enough in that knowledge to be a servant. Here was a demonstration of an attitude so radical we still struggle with it today.

I can think of few better examples in the New Testament that illustrate the point Jesus is making in our text, "Blessed are the poor in spirit." He gives us that security. He says, "If you'll be Mine, I'll make you like that." It's not a matter of trying to act like this so we can "make it into the kingdom." Here Jesus says, "As you let Me be in control in your life, I'll help you see your worth. I'll help you see your value. I'll help you see how important you are. You can expect that to happen."

And then Christians who see themselves walking in God's story can walk into a roomful of people, or stand up front before the church, and instead of thinking to themselves, *I wonder what people are thinking of me,* can muse, *I wonder how God would like to use me in the lives of these people today.*

It was my privilege for many years to teach young preachers how to preach. One of the great dilemmas every one of them faced, almost without exception, was stage fright. One day one of them said, "I know this is going to be a good speech—my knees are applauding already."

But Christian maturity helps us move beyond *I wonder what people are going to think of me today* to the point where we can say, *I wonder how God would like to use me in the lives of these people this morning.* The focus can shift from us to how God wants to use us for His purposes.

Let me tell you about Paul Hopkins. He will be embarrassed when he reads this, but it is a story that needs to be told.

Adventist World Radio (AWR) was looking for someone to give leadership to our direct mail program. This is the plan by which we tell our broadcast partners about how God is leading in this ministry and then solicit their prayers and financial support. It is a key role in Adventist World Radio. We hired Paul for the job, even though he had just graduated from college.

I remember well the first time we sat together in my

office to discuss his duties. He was very eager to please, to be successful, to become a valued part of Team AWR, as we like to call it. He wanted to know exactly what I expected and how he could meet the expectations. He wanted to prove he could do a good job.

But during the months that followed there was an interesting change in Paul. I began to notice that our conversations were changing. Instead of talking about how he might satisfy the job description, Paul began to talk about our listeners, about the deep gratitude he was developing toward those whose regular gifts and earnest prayers keep our broadcasts on the air. The focus moved conspicuously away from a self-conscious desire to please to a mature desire to be helpful.

More than once he came to the office aglow with a statement he had just read in his private devotional time. Inevitably he would already be thinking about how he could send it to our supporters. Rather than investing his energies in wondering how he could meet his professional goals, he was developing a heart hunger to be of value to God's kingdom.

What a remarkable, liberating transformation that can be. God takes the humble clay of humanity and elevates us to the privilege of being part of His great redemptive strategy for the planet. Now, that'll make you smile. Talk about a call to joy!

Our Wonderful Inability to Help Ourselves

And that brings up my third statement about this beatitude: True joy comes only to those who discover their inability to help themselves. In a very real sense this is what it means to be "poor in spirit." It does not mean to be long-faced and downcast. It means to be aware of our inadequacies and vividly conscious of the fact that we are utterly unable to help ourselves in any way that affects our attractiveness or worthiness before God. Simply stated, it brings joy to discover not only that we can't make it on our own, but that we don't have to!

It is no accident that Jesus included this statement at the very beginning of the Sermon on the Mount. This was not an afterthought, an incidental postscript to His message to us. There was a reason Jesus started with this concept. Basic to our understanding of what it means to be Christian is a realization that we cannot help ourselves.

Yet we struggle to grasp this concept. We are so individualistic and achievement-oriented, especially in the American culture. After all, the Bible says, "God helps them that help themselves," right? Wrong! I can't count the number of times I've heard people quote that "scripture" to me. But even though it's not scriptural at all, it fits our human estimate of what Scripture ought to say, since we're so caught up in what we can do. But it is not what God has to say to us.

We come by this powerful achievement orientation right from the beginning of our lives, even in our families. For example, think back to your own dinner table as you were growing up. How did you qualify for dessert after a meal? You had to clean up your plate.

At Christmas, to whom does "Santa Claus" bring the gifts? To good little boys and girls, of course. At church, the way you get the gold star on your chart is to learn your memory verse. At school the way you get from the eighth grade into the ninth grade is to do the work. And on the job the way you get the raise is to produce.

All through our lives we're conditioned to believe that the only way we get anything is to earn it. Then God comes along and says, "I've got something for you that's free, and there's nothing you can do to deserve it." Is it any surprise that it challenges us to understand and to live that way?

Let me ask you a question. Which comes first to a new believer, privilege or responsibility? The correct answer is that privilege comes first. The privilege of basking in forgiveness, of accepting something I did not earn, of knowing that forgiveness is mine when He had no just reason to give it to me. After that, responsibilities follow. But privileges come first, and that's the heart of this message.

"Blessed are the poor in spirit." Blessed are those who realize that they can do nothing to help themselves. In the transaction of forgiveness, it is all one-sided.

But what about the practical implications? Does that mean that we go on and live as we please?

Of course not—if what that means is to go on and live in a way that is contrary to God's will. Jesus did not rescue us to live "in" our sins; He rescued us "from" them so we could experience all the joy He intended for us. The transaction that makes me whole in the sight of God is not something I deserve or something I can earn in any way.

We're exploring now something that is really basic in the Christian experience. You see, the devil would like to have us set out to work on our sins—to get up in the morning and say "OK, I'm not going to lose my temper today. I'm *not* going to lose my temper today." That sounds very religious, like something we all ought to be doing; but it is really spiritually destructive. Why? Because all day long—in this mind-set—we're focusing on not losing our temper. We spend the day living sin-centered lives because we are working on that one thing we want to get rid of.

Have you heard the story about the trader who went to the South Seas? The people who were living there would make handicrafts and he would buy these things from them, take them back to his country, and sell them. One day he went to the island and said, "I'm not just going to pay you in gold; I'm going to teach you how to make gold."

"Oh," they said, "this is wonderful. We'll be the wealthiest people in the islands."

So he said, "Now, get a big pot and build a fire under it. You put in water and the juice from these berries and some ground-up roots and crocodile teeth and so forth. Then you say this magic formula over it while the water boils."

Well, when no one was looking he slipped some gold nuggets in the pot. And afterward they pulled the pot off the fire and poured out all the water, and there, in the bottom, were some nuggets of gold.

"Oh," they enthused, "this is wonderful. We're wealthy!"

Then he said, "Now, there's just one thing I need to tell you. All the time the fire is burning, you must not think about the red-faced monkey, or it won't work!"

The next time they got the water and the fire and the pot and the juice and the berries and all the rest together, but when they poured the water off afterward, there was no gold. "All right, who was it?" they asked. "Who was thinking about the red-faced monkey?"

The devil would like to have us concentrate on those "red-faced monkeys," those sins that so easily beset us, so that we live sin-centered lives instead of Christ-centered lives.

Jesus says, "Acknowledge that there is nothing you can do to help yourself. There is nothing you can do to forgive your own sins, to merit My pleasure. Nothing. But spend that time with Me, expose yourself to My Word. Come on; let's talk. Submit those decisions to My lordship, and I'll make you like that. My life will come into yours; I'll live within. And when My character begins to be reproduced in your life—as that experience grows and develops and matures—those sinful tendencies will begin to drop away like leaves off a tree in the autumn."

And so Jesus says, "Blessed are the poor in spirit." He describes as "happy" the person who has discovered not only that they cannot save themselves but that they don't have to. What a liberating relief!

The key word in a Christian experience is "dependence": moment by moment, hour by hour, every day. He does for me what I cannot do for myself. He says, "I wanted happiness for you, but you lost it through disobedience. You walked away from Me. You broke the connection. But I have the power and the will to reconnect with you. Remember, sorrow and sighing and those things that make life unpleasant are going to flee away. The happiness that I have for you is eternal."

Why? "Because I love you." We call it grace—amazing grace!

Maybe, then, we could paraphrase this first beatitude in these words: "Those who sense their total dependence on God and allow Him to do His transforming work in them are the happiest people in the world."

You want that kind of happiness, don't you? I know I do. We can't get it by seeking it. We can get it only by accepting God's great gift and allowing Him to become a vital presence in our lives. I know, it seems too good to be true. But that's what the gospel is: God's message that's too good to be true—but is!

LISTENING TO GOD: THOUGHT QUESTIONS

☛ Do you believe that you can ever find true happiness through clinging to your pride? Don't most of the difficulties we face day to day come from circumstances in which we let pride rule us?

☞ When someone tries to affirm you in some way, how do you react? Are you embarrassed? Have you considered an intentional response that accepts the affirmation, yet doesn't feed pride? What might such a response be?

☞ If we're culturally programmed to tie everything to performance, how does the Christian ever learn to accept God's gift? Is it possible for us to separate faith from efforts to earn God's acceptance? What happens if we're never able to make that break?

SHARING WITH GOD: THE MINISTRY OF PRAYER

Lord, so often when I try to see Your face I find myself staring at my own reflection. So often when I try to accept Your grace I find myself still working to earn whatever You do for me. Intellectually I understand that You love me and have redeemed me, totally separate from my own efforts. Yet my faith is so small.

"Help me to accept Your love for me at face value. Help me to see my own worth through Your eyes. Help me to value others in the same way that You value me.

"And give me the courage to translate all that into accepting, redemptive actions that allow You to use me effectively. Give me the boldness to be Your person in the place You've set me.

"Amen."

3 | Happy Mourners

Blessed are those who mourn, for they shall be comforted (Matt. 5:4, RSV).

This is one of the greatest paradoxes in Scripture: "Happy are the sad." That's rather like saying "Hot are the cold." Have you ever wondered what Jesus meant by this seemingly contradictory statement? Have you ever wished you were in the crowd as He spoke that day, so you could raise your hand, ever so tentatively, and say, "Um, I'm sorry to interrupt, Jesus, but just what do You mean by 'Happy are the sad'? I don't want to seem argumentative or anything, but You really lost me on this one. How can you be happy if you're not happy?"

As we've seen before in this amazing sermon, here we have another statement of great significance, great meaning, great richness. But it is troubling until we look below the surface. This is true with much of what Jesus said. In fact, He told the disciples that He spoke in parables because He didn't want everything He said to be obvious.

Many times I've had people—especially college and seminary students—ask me why the Bible isn't more simple. Why isn't it just laid out so anyone can pick it up and understand it? I'm sure I don't know all of the reasons God chose to cloak some of it in mystery and symbolism, but let me make an observation. It has been interesting to watch how often the search for truth deepens commitment. More often than we know, a man or woman comes to the Word of God seeking to get better acquainted with Him, and it is the search that does it. As they pray and ponder, read and consider, explore and think, they discover truths they didn't even know existed. And I believe that's what is going to happen here.

Now, obviously, Jesus is not calling us to a lifetime of moroseness and melancholy. He was not that kind of person Himself, and He surely wouldn't want us to be.

Hearts Broken by the Things That Break God's Heart

Sadness is hatched from many different kinds of eggs. We can be sad because of mistakes we or others have made. We can be sad because of things others have done to us that make us feel betrayed or abused. Sadness comes when we don't meet expectations others set for us or that we set for ourselves, or when we suffer some wrenching loss.

The mourners Jesus is describing here, however, are quite different. They are those who have allowed their hearts to be broken by the things that break the heart of God.

What breaks God's heart?

Well, since Jesus best exemplifies the character of God, with a heart that was touched as God's heart is touched, we can ask, "What broke Jesus' heart?" And in the Gospel account of the life of Christ we have some very specific answers.

There are two accounts in the Gospel record of times that Jesus wept. The first is the brief story that contains the shortest verse in Scripture. It's found in John 11.

This incident took place in the village of Bethany, where Lazarus, a friend of Jesus', was ill. The sisters of Lazarus sent word to Jesus: "Your friend is sick. Won't You please come and heal him?" These sisters were believers who had faith in God's miracle-working power. They not only believed Jesus could heal their brother, they believed He would.

The messenger arrived, but for some strange reason Jesus did not immediately respond to the sisters' request. He continued ministering where He was, seemingly ignoring the plight of His friends. And in the meantime, as Jesus delayed, Lazarus died.

Now, here's the dilemma: As long as there is life there is hope. But Mary and Martha must have been distraught as they watched their brother become increasingly ill. They did not have access to medical science as we do, and simple things could turn into life-threatening situations quickly. That illness, whatever it was, became a big-time crisis, and their beloved brother died—right there in their home. What a huge cloud of despair must have settled over that house! They had trusted that Jesus would come and save His friend. But He didn't show up.

Four days would pass before Jesus would appear. Paint the picture in your mind as He approaches their home in Bethany. "Then Mary, when she came where Jesus was and saw him, fell at his feet, saying to him, 'Lord, if you had been here, my brother would not have died.' When Jesus saw her weeping, and the Jews who came with her also weeping, he was deeply moved in spirit and troubled; and he said, 'Where have you laid him?' They said to him, 'Lord, come and see.' Jesus wept. So the Jews said, 'See how he loved him!'" (John 11:32-36, RSV).

Why did Jesus weep when He received word of the

death of His friend Lazarus? Was it because He was going to miss stopping by Lazarus' place for a free meal now and then? Was it because He would miss the long talks He and Lazarus used to have?

Perhaps, but I believe Jesus cried because He was touched by the deep anguish that the people He loved were feeling. I believe it's because here, perhaps more than at any other time, there was pressed upon His heart the way that death and separation stab anguish into the heart of the human family.

When you and I lay a loved one down in the valley of the shadow, we can know that we do not walk through that valley alone. Jesus has been there. He knows what it's like. He knows the anguish that sin brings to the human heart. This second beatitude is calling us to invest our hearts in the agony around us.

Let me describe a problem that I see.

We don't read very far into the Scripture record before we discover that God wants His people to be different from the people in the world around them—separate in some very profound ways. So when we choose a place to live, as much as is possible, we take that into account. We want it to be a place that assists us in this distinctiveness, not one that makes it harder. We're separate in the forms of recreation we choose too. We're willing to be different, not taking part in what's going on around us if it would compromise our spiritual integrity.

That attitude carries over into such decisions as what we eat, how we dress—in fact, to about everything we do, even including the support of an expensive separate educational system for our church. The principle of being separate from "the world" as a Christian is clear, and the reasons for it are thoroughly defensible.

But while Christians walk in the world and must not be contaminated by its sinfulness, neither must they allow themselves to be insulated from its heartache. It's very easy for us to miss the point here and use our separateness as a form of hiding, a form of protecting ourselves from being where God wants us to be.

We decry world conditions that create poverty and inequality, but we make our complaints from the depths of our carpeted living rooms. Then, dressed in our church best and smelling clean, we go to worship in beautiful stone sanctuaries with lovely landscaping and paved parking lots so we won't get dust on our shined shoes. We sit on padded pews, in air-conditioned comfort. And as the sunlight pours through our stained-glass windows, we sing to the stirring strains of a majestic organ, "Rescue the Perishing."

I remember visiting one of our churches on the island of Madagascar, off the southeastern coast of Africa. We slithered cautiously over rutted, muddy roads for two hours till we ran out of navigable terrain. There we parked the Jeep and walked for more than an hour.

I don't know what I was expecting, but I was surprised. We were met by a young family who had accepted Christ through listening to our AWR broadcasts. They were so thankful for the message of salvation that they built a church. It was humble enough—dirt floor, tin roof, benches with no backs. But it was their gift to God.

As we talked to them through an interpreter, they told us about conditions in their village, about the sickness, a recent death, the poor education, and the hopelessness of those who had no faith in Christ. It was not difficult to realize that this precious family was living in the midst of great need, and they knew it. They saw their church as more of a jungle clinic than an architectural statement.

Now, I'm not suggesting for a moment that we tear down our churches because they look too nice. I am not suggesting that we are wrong to want to protect our families. I'm saying only that it is difficult to live in a spirit of concern when we're so comfortable.

A Prescription

First of all, I'd like to suggest that one of our keys here must be to shun the artificial. May I be a bit impertinent and talk about television? It is my observation that there is no other single influence that is having the effect on the Christian home today that television is. None. Not parents, not the church, not the school. I invite you to think carefully through this issue with me. I know it isn't a popular topic with some, but it's my sense that we need to talk about it.

We could talk about the 18,000 murders that happen in the living room of typical American youngsters before they go away to college. Or the casual way in which Hollywood is attempting to make homosexuality acceptable. We could talk about the violence, the sexual promiscuity, the language, and the utter nonsense of so much of it.

But I believe there is something even more sinister for the Christian whose goal is to develop the traits of Christlikeness. We develop what I like to call an emotional callus. We immerse ourselves in the artificial until the real loses its effect. The special-effects wizards ply their trade with such skill that our palms get sweaty, our hands get clammy, and we can feel our hearts beating—and the next time it doesn't have quite the same emotional wallop. Emotional callouses.

We're talking about staying sensitive to the hurts of a world gone mad, about allowing our hearts to be broken by the things that break the heart of God.

Further, it may be helpful at times to design our own intentional exposure to a hurting world. For instance, once I went to visit a little boy in the children's hospital near where we were living in Atlanta. I couldn't help noticing that just across the hall was a little girl, 9 months old, with a pin through her left leg, in traction. She had been lying on her back in that little bed for six weeks. She was a beautiful baby, and as I stood there I found myself asking, "Dear God, how long is it going to be before this kind of thing is over?"

In the next room was a little boy with a malformation of the spine. I think the nurse called it spina bifida. It was an emotional half hour.

As I walked those hallways, as I looked in those rooms, it reminded me of a story my friend Roland Hegstad told. One day he received a phone call from some people whose little daughter, on her way home from school, was picked up by a man and woman and forced into their car. The man raped that little 7-year-old girl in the back seat, and then his wife reached over the seat and clubbed her to death with a tire iron.

Pastor Hegstad was called on to conduct the funeral. As he told the story, he said, "I stood beside that family, looking down into the face of that little 7-year-old girl, who grew up and grew old and died all in the space of a half hour. And I said to myself, 'Dear God, if by my lethargy, by my lukewarmness, I let this miserable world go on five minutes longer than it has to, how am I going to answer to You on the judgment day?'"

Visit a divorce court. Sit in the back row and just listen as a grown man and a grown woman fight over a boat and a silver tea set while their two children cling to each other in the second row.

HAPPY MOURNERS

Take your children with you and sit in the waiting area of the emergency room of a nearby hospital on a holiday weekend. Watch and listen to the painful drama that unfolds there.

Visit a rescue mission, as my wife and I did a while ago in Chicago, and see the men and the women sitting there, waiting. Vacant stares; no tomorrow. It's hard to be complacent and comfortable when that kind of genuine anguish is real before your eyes.

I wish I could introduce you to a friend of mine from East Africa whom I will call Ahmad. When he became a Christian he had to flee his country and leave behind his five children and his wife, who was pregnant with their sixth child. In his country it is against the law to leave the state religion and become a Christian, and a neighbor told him that people from the town were coming that night to kill him.

Ahmad walked and hitchhiked for two days, sleeping in trees at night trying to get protection from the rain. He finally reached the safety of a neighboring country, but was treated as a refugee and placed in a camp. He lived there for six months, without his family and with no sanitary facilities, meager food, and rampant sickness among the 4,000 others who were there. When I met him he was gaunt from hunger, but joyous that he had been released and not sent back to his own country.

For weeks he tried to make covert contact with his family. By this time his wife had delivered their sixth child, and Ahmad didn't even know if it was a boy or a girl. In time Ahmad's family was able to leave their home country too, but then all of them were sent to the squalor of "the camp." In his halting English, with pleading eyes, he tried to explain to me how terrible it was to live there. Even though his faith in God was strong, he could hardly stand the pain of seeing his wife and children in those circumstances.

I thought, *Oh, God, I wish I could change it for him. I wish I could take them all out of there. I wish I could find them a nice place to live with a green lawn for the children to play on and clean water for them to drink.*

It is very difficult to come face to face with the horrible results of life on a sinful planet and not be changed by them. Without Jesus that exposure can result in disillusionment and despair. But with Jesus it can transform us and give us hearts that are touched by the things that touch the heart of God.

The second time it is recorded that Jesus cried is in Matthew 23. This chapter not only contains His scathing rebukes to the Pharisees but also exposes His passionate heart. Near the end, in verse 37, as He stands overlooking the city of Jerusalem, with tears running down His cheeks, He says, "O Jerusalem, Jerusalem, you who kill the prophets and stone those sent to you, how often I have longed to gather your children together, as a hen gathers her chicks under her wings, but you were not willing" (NIV).

You see, the heart of Jesus is also broken by the reality of eternal loss. It is an unbearable thought to Him that some of those He loves will choose not to accept the eternal salvation He offers.

How about you? What thoughts and feelings are generated when you fly over the great cities of our world or drive their crowded highways? Is it road rage over the actions of some other driver, or outrage that the devil has been successful in deluding a whole generation into turning their backs on God's incredible offer?

Walk intently in God's story. The more closely we walk with Him, the more our hearts beat in unison.

Our human inclination is to develop what I call a final exam syndrome. Here is how it works: We slough along during the semester, figuring that the last thing before exams we'll really cram and learn all we need to know, because the important thing is to get through the final exam, pass the course, and get the diploma. Well, that may work with education, but that's really bargain-basement religion for the Christian.

It's a great temptation to keep an eye on the sand as it is running through the hourglass and hope that the signs of the times and our bad habits run out about the same time. But whether I think Jesus is coming tomorrow or a hundred years from now should not make a bit of difference in the way I live. If it does, then I'm just playing games. I'm really saying, "I want to live selfishly. I want to live my way. I want to make my own decisions. But I want to make sure I get the retirement policy at the end."

Going Beyond Squelching Our Temptations

The question is not how we can sit on the lid of our temptations and squeak into the kingdom, but rather how we can nurture a loathing for sin that makes us consistently victorious Christians—"more than conquerors," as Paul says in Romans 8:37. A phrase in one of our beloved Christian hymns entreats, "Take away our bent to sinning." That's it. That's what we want to have happen. Let's talk about how.

Through communion with God, sin becomes hateful to us. It really is that simple. This is one of the most profound insights in all of Christianity. Our goal is not to see how much we can learn to hate sin, but to discover how much we can learn to love God. As our love for Him deepens He changes us, and hatred for sin is the inevitable result.

So in this important beatitude Jesus says, "The mourners I am speaking of are those whose hearts have been broken by the things that break the heart of God." Therefore, the key to making this come true in us is to look into God's heart.

The pattern we see is a consistent one. There, in the Garden of Eden, watch as God calls that frolicking lamb to His side. And watch as He takes its life to make a covering for Adam and Eve.

What do you suppose that did to God's heart?

Or stand there at the gate with Him as He points down that path and says to Adam and Eve, "You must go now," knowing as only God could know what sin would do to human hearts for 6,000 years. Watch as with great agony of soul He opens the fountains of the deep to destroy a whole world.

Or there, at Calvary. His Son, who has been sent to love the human race, to heal their bodies, to feed them, to touch their tongues and make them speak, to touch their ears and make them hear, to restore sight to their eyes, is now impaled on a cross. You'd think people would be standing in line to get into His church. Instead they spit in His face. And surely God wept.

As you and I look on, we weep also in sorrow, in embarrassment, and in joy because now we know: Happy are those whose sins have driven them to Christ, where they have found the reality of His forgiveness. They have allowed their hearts to be broken by those things that have broken the heart of God. He is implanting His character in their hearts, and there can be no greater joy.

***

LISTENING TO GOD: THOUGHT QUESTIONS

☞ The basic theme of this chapter is allowing ourselves to be touched by the same things that touch the heart of

God. Do you think it is possible for mere humans to feel about sin the same way God does? What is different about the way we see sin from the way God sees it?

☞ We've suggested in this chapter a couple ways we can have our hearts reshaped. One of them is through shunning the artificial. Besides television, what other artificial things fill our lives that we might reconsider?

☞ Another suggestion in the chapter is to expose ourselves intentionally to a hurting world. What are some specific ways we could do this? Is this something we should do occasionally, or are there some ways we can do this on a continuing basis?

☞ The chapter makes an important distinction between working to hate sin and working to love God. What could we do in our lives to help us love God more?

SHARING WITH GOD: THE MINISTRY OF PRAYER

Lord, I am often a victim of my own good intentions. I want to be more like You, and I make occasional real efforts in that direction; however, the harder I work at being good, it seems the more I just become like the people around me.

"Would You send Your Spirit to me in the middle of my real everyday life as I try to remake myself, to whisper to me with Your warm loving voice? Would You remind me that I need to look to You, not to myself?

"And would You give me an extra measure of courage, so I'll be willing to see the things You want to show me about the pain and suffering sin causes? I pray that You'll transform my heart, so I can be touched as You are and feel the same compassion You feel, so I then can be used in the ways You want to use me.

"Thank You for allowing me to be part of what You are doing in the world.

"Amen."

Does That Mean I'm Supposed to Be Bashful?

Blessed are the meek for they shall inherit the earth. Matt. 5:5, RSV.

Blessed are the meek." I'd like to take that phrase to a sign painter and have it put on a big poster. Maybe painted in bright red, so everybody would see it. Now, let's see, what shall we do with it? I wonder where we might take it?

How about the locker room of the Minnesota Vikings at halftime? Lift up the sign: "Blessed are the meek." Maybe we should approach the players, dirty and sweaty, and say, "Guys, we were just wondering . . . we saw you in a circle on your knees, praying before the game—so you must be Christians. Now, we were curious about when the coach gets you all together to plan strategy for the second half. Is he going to talk about displaying more meekness? It doesn't seem as though that's the mood in the locker room, but maybe we're missing something."

What do you think? Would my sign find a responsive audience? Perhaps not.

DOES THAT MEAN I'M SUPPOSED TO BE BASHFUL?

Well, maybe we ought to take it to the United States National Security Council as they're discussing the threat of terrorism in this country. Lift up the sign: "Blessed are the meek." We could suggest, "Pardon me, but when you're planning your strategy for dealing with future attacks on U.S. naval vessels, be sure to take into account the need for our people to stay properly meek—especially those CIA agents." Or we could advise, "How about some meekness training? I know a good seminar leader I could recommend." I don't know, but I doubt they'd take that suggestion very seriously.

How about the delegates to the Middle East peace talks? Lift up the sign: "Blessed are the meek." Should we give the Jewish and Palestinian leaders a lecture on meekness? "Now, come on, folks, you represent two of the world's great religions. Why all this talk about threats and violence? Don't you understand anything about meekness? You're supposed to know this stuff!" Somehow, I don't think that's an arena in which any of the people assembled would find our remarks appealing, either.

Well, maybe we could just put it on a street corner in the inner city somewhere. Lift up the sign: "Blessed are the meek." We could shout, "Hey, everybody, we're having a 'meek-in' this week. Everybody is invited. Bring along the meekest person you know!" I have a hunch people might just walk by and snicker.

Maybe we could put it in the boardroom of General Motors. Lift up the sign: "Blessed are the meek." We could hold a seminar on the bottom-line benefits from meekness, or suggest a new ad campaign that features it: "Buy a Chevy Camaro and get 1,000 Meek Points toward winning a new Corvette! Five hundred bonus points if you buy a convertible."

CALL TO JOY

You know, it seems as though that "Blessed are the meek" sign is not going to be very popular in government, in sports, in business—or about anywhere we want to put it. It's a nuisance. In fact, it's becoming a downright embarrassment.

"Blessed are the meek." Whose idea was this, anyway?

If you browse through any bookstore today, you'll find that meekness is completely out of sync with what's being written for the popular press. You can buy all kinds of books on assertiveness training. How to say no. How to control people. How to get your own way. Some time back I got a book in the mail entitled *Pastoral Assertiveness*. The idea is that a pastor is supposed to assert himself or herself and not be run over by the congregation. I haven't read it yet. I may, though.

We are barraged with messages different from "Blessed are the meek." But if we think it's out of step now, think of how it must have jarred the people who heard it when Jesus spoke it.

The Jews were in bondage. An army of occupation had moved in. God's people were under the control of the Romans. The Jewish people were looking desperately for somebody to come as a military deliverer and free them. It would be as if Saddam Hussein had won the Gulf War and then moved on to conquer the United States. All Americans would be meeting in secret, praying that some charismatic military genius would arise and deliver them from these foreign intruders.

In Jesus' day every time a new zealot arose, the people would begin to have a glimmer of hope. They would whisper, "Maybe our new military deliverer is here now."

When Jesus came on the scene, they weren't sure about Him, but they knew, at least, that He had galvanized the attention of the people. People were listening; they were following Him by the thousands. And now He gathers this great assemblage in front of Him and begins to talk to them about the kingdom He's come to establish.

I can envision some in the crowd having come to the meeting in the hope that Jesus would be the deliverer. Before coming, they'd talked about it back home in whispered tones.

"He might be the one, you know."

"No, I don't think so. Where's his army?"

"I don't know. Maybe He'll train us and arm us, and we can be the army."

"But Rome is so powerful."

"Any army can be beat."

Now they're here, standing in the crowd.

"He's not much to look at," one of them whispers as they mill about the edges of the crowd, wanting to see, but careful not to be seen. "See, there are His disciples, helping to seat people. None of them look like soldiers."

"Shh," another man says. "He's getting ready to speak. Can't you just feel the power in Him? This is going to be great!"

But then, imagine how stunned—how crushed—they are when Jesus says, "Blessed are the meek." That is not what they want to hear. How can you build a revolution around meekness? They want Jesus to issue a call to arms!

But there it is: "Blessed are the meek."

Let's be practical. Isn't it usually the aggressive person who wins in life? It's the aggressive salesperson who gets the big order, not the Caspar Milquetoast. It's the one who's out there beating the bushes and saying, "Here's my product! This is the one you've been needing! It's better than anybody else's!" Isn't it the aggressive salesperson who gets to be district manager?

You want to be a leader, don't you? Someone who can motivate the sales force to sell more and achieve great things. Someone who can stand up and say, "Follow me!" and they do. Do you get there by exercising the trait of meekness?

Let's move this discussion out of the business world. Isn't it the aggressive church that makes an impact on the community? Isn't it the aggressive pastor who has the baptisms at the end of the year? Don't our powers of observation demonstrate that it's strong leadership that makes men and women successful and effective? Doesn't this simple statement from Jesus fly in the face of all that we see? How practical is this "meekness" idea, anyway? Does what Jesus said really work?

Will the Real Meek People Please Stand Up?

Perhaps it's an injustice to contrast "meek" with "aggressive." I think we're missing something. Maybe those are not opposite ends of the spectrum. Let's spend a minute defining what Jesus meant when He used the word "meek." After all, meekness is an attribute that is consistently described in Scripture as being desirable. Moses is commended for being the meekest man who ever lived. And God said of that trait in him, "That's good."

Meekness is one of the fruits of the Spirit in Galatians 5:22, 23. That means if the Spirit lives within, He'll help us to become like that. In 1 Peter 3, Christian women are encouraged not to try to paint beauty on the outside, but rather to develop the true beauty that comes from the inside—that of a meek and quiet spirit. And in that same passage it says that a meek spirit is, in the sight of God, of great price.

Jesus said of Himself that He was meek and lowly in

heart, and He invited us to become like Him (Matt. 11:29).

With this kind of background, it's obvious that this was not just a flippant, offhanded, unrehearsed statement. In fact, Jesus was referring to Psalm 37. Meekness is standard operating procedure for a Christian. It's not just for that select few who were born with a gentle disposition and who don't mind being pushed around by the world.

Let me ask you, Does to be meek mean to be without courage? Does meek mean weak?

Well, it's easy to answer that. Let's stand here behind this pillar for a minute and watch that rather tall Stranger walk into the Temple. See Him walk up to that little table with a calculator and a cash box on it and push the whole thing over, dumping it right into the lap of the man who's sitting there. Then He goes to the next little table and does the same thing. And another, and another. And in the hushed awe that follows, you hear little else but coins rolling across the hard stone floor.

It is Jesus. Gentle Jesus, meek and mild.

Now, you might think He could get away with that once, using the element of surprise. But months later He came back and did it again. No. To be meek does not mean to be without courage.

Let me ask you another question, and perhaps this shatters the stereotype most effectively of all: Does to be meek mean to be timid and bashful? Usually when we conjure up a mental image of a meek person, it's a timid little shadow in the corner.

Sit here on this stone for a minute and watch that suntanned, muscular, bearded patriarch walking there in the distance, as he makes his way down the side of that great stone mountain. Watch him now as he stands before the whole nation. There are at least a million people, maybe 5 million. Listen to his irrepressible words as he rebukes them for their apostasy. Then he takes that gold statue of a cow around which they have been dancing, throws it in the fire, and when it melts down he grinds up the gold, dumps it in their drinking water, and makes them drink it.

This is Moses, the meekest man who ever lived.

To be meek does not mean to be timid and bashful. What then does it mean to be meek?

"Meek" was a common word in the Greek language. It meant to tame a wild animal. I like that imagery. The animal was no less strong, but its destructive energy had been rechanneled and was now usable for constructive purposes.

When "meek" was used to describe a person, it meant one who had been gentled and quieted. It described someone whose natural forcefulness had not been destroyed but had been redirected. The lion had not been killed, only tamed.

A couple years ago one of our AWR representatives went to visit a listener in central Brazil. It was not easy to locate the woman who had written, because addresses in that part of the world are somewhat imprecise. But after a while our worker got directions.

The listener, it turned out, was a woman of some influence in the community. In fact, since she had been listening to our programs she had begun to organize regular times when many of her neighbors would gather together at her home and listen with her.

Our visiting worker spent parts of two days there helping to nurture this budding Christian community. Before he left, he and the woman had a long conversation about her faith in Christ and how it had changed her. She wanted to be baptized, and she wanted to help influence her village to accept Christ. As they were ending their conversation she gave this interesting testimony: "The thing that brings me the greatest happiness is that since accepting Jesus I have been able to quit beating my husband."

People who are meek no longer need to use their forcefulness to defend their pride or to insist on having their own way. Now all of the intensity and enthusiasm with which God endows us at birth is made available to accomplish God's purposes instead of our own. Meekness is strength grown tender. It is might—with a caress in its brawny hands.

The power is not in the thunder. You and I have both seen people who, behind a smoke screen of noise and loud talk and swearing, were hiding some pretty insecure feelings. The power is not in the noise. It is strength that can afford to be gentle.

A Christian is not meek because he or she is weak. Meekness is not impotence. A Christian is meek because he or she chooses to be controlled. They may still be forceful—but at the right time and at the right place and for the right reasons. The people in Scripture who are called meek were often very forceful. But they were forceful in defending God's honor, not their own.

Maybe the best way to get a handle on meekness is to watch it at work. Look at Genesis 13:1-9. "So Abram went up from Egypt, he and his wife, and all that he had, and Lot with him, into the Negeb [or into the desert, into the wilderness]. Now Abram was very rich in cattle, in silver, and in gold. And he journeyed on from the Negeb as far as Bethel, to the place where his tent had been at the beginning, between Bethel and Ai, to the place where he had made an altar at the first; and there Abram called on the name of the Lord. And Lot, who went with Abram, also had flocks and herds and tents, so that the land could not support both of them dwelling together; for their possessions were so great that they could not dwell together, and there was strife between the herdsmen of Abram's cattle and the herdsmen of Lot's cattle. . . .

"Then Abram said to Lot, 'Let there be no strife between you and me, and between your herdsmen and my herdsmen; for we are kinsmen. Is not the whole land before you? Separate yourself from me. If you take the left hand, then I will go to the right; or if you take the right hand, then I will go to the left'" (RSV).

Abraham and Lot have come to a place where their herds are so vast that there's not enough pasture all in one place. And there's strife as the herdsmen are quarreling over who gets the better pasture. Abraham could have said to Lot, "Now look, God promised me that this property would be mine. I'm the one who received the covenant. You're only a hitchhiking relative. I'm going to take this great fertile plain. You go find yourself some pasture somewhere else."

If he had said that, it would have been true—and most would have judged it fair. But instead Abraham said, "Look, there's not enough grass here for your cattle and mine. I'll tell you what, let's divide it up. You take whatever you want, and I'll take what's left."

You see, meekness does not ask, "What are my rights?" Meekness asks, "What is the loving thing to do?"

Meekness is strength grown tender. What a concept! But what would it mean to me if I allowed God to make me meek?

How Does Meekness Play Out in Real Life?

Genuine Christianity has always been counterculture. God's people have always marched out of step with the world around them. And when we consider allowing God to transform us, we need to be aware of just how radical that transformation might be.

Does that mean that the Christian is willing to be taken advantage of in business? Maybe.

"But that's not right," you argue. "That's not reasonable."

Reasonableness. Interesting idea. We need to come face to face with the different reality Jesus proposes for us. Some of the things Jesus said do not answer to an appeal to fairness as the world defines it. And some of them don't fit well onto the scale of reasonableness—because the more the Spirit of God lives within us, the more our values become unearthly. When we say—as we do in this book—that this is His call to a radical way of life, that's exactly the case. As we become His, we move away from what we are by nature to something entirely different.

I don't know about you, but the more time I spend with these dynamic insights, the more I realize that only as He lives in me can I become what Jesus wants me to be.

When Jesus says, "Blessed are the meek," He is not just talking about how we respond to those who are nice to us. He's not just talking about a trait that is developed in us when we are born into a home in which we learn gracious manners. He's not just asking us to be thoughtful of others and socially proper. This is a radical call to a different way to live. It's a trait that can be developed only by the Holy Spirit. It is an attitude that allows for no resentment, no retaliation, no bitterness.

That's tough, isn't it? We're not like that. It's a million miles from our natural way of behaving. I'm willing to say, "I am a sinner," but I don't want anybody else saying amen to that. And what about when we're criticized or condemned or put down? How should we react? Listen: meekness weeps more for the wrongdoer than for its own wounds. That's a startling thought. It reaches deeply into my heart and touches something powerful. Those who are truly meek are more saddened by seeing the way sin twists the mind and warps the heart of the one who strikes out at them than they are by the hurt they themselves endure. What a transformation!

Here's another radical idea tied to meekness: It is a greater show of strength for a person of strong and tempestuous temper to demonstrate control when provoked than it is to lash out and throw a chair. Going with your anger is the easy thing. Redirecting your anger into something productive and transforming is far harder—and intimately tied to the development of true meekness.

Now let's get down-home practical: How does all this work out at home? Let's say a husband's leadership in his home is challenged, maybe by a wayward child or a crotchety wife. The husband's tendency is to lash out, to react, to make a lot of noise, to demand some respect. Instead of that, meekness leads that man to the bedroom, where, on his knees beside his bed, he prays something like this: "Dear God, what is it in my life that makes it difficult for You to exercise leadership in my family through me?"

When Moses, who we've already said was the meekest man who ever lived, was confronted with a rebellious people, he responded in two ways. On one occasion he lost his temper, and that was serious enough to God that—for that act—he was kept out of the Promised Land. The other way in which he responded to rebellion was to go to the tabernacle and plead in humility that God would reinstitute His leadership in those people through him, Moses. And only when he did that did God deal with the rebellion.

"OK," you respond, "but what if my wife was wrong in what she said?"

Do you remember a New Testament statement that

says that husbands are to love their wives as Christ loved the church? Jesus loved the church even when she was rebellious and even in her rebellion; He went the way of the cross for her. So if a husband is to love his wife as Christ loved the church, even in her rebellion, he is to go the way of the cross. He is to take the initiative.

But what does that mean? Taking the initiative does not entitle the husband to say, "OK, now I did my part. The rest is up to you." He is responsible only for his own attitude. He is not conscience for her. Meekness says, "Forgive me for what I said; forgive me for what I did." And if her attitude is not one of forgiveness in return, that is not part of the condition. He is to do what he is to do without requiring of her what she is to do.

Husbands, love your wives as Christ loves the church— powerfully, sacrificially, and unilaterally. An attitude of meekness says, "I will bring myself to her, crucified if need be, and ask her forgiveness."

Women, what about the times your husband is unfair? The attitude of the Christian wife, Jesus said, is to be one of meekness. How does meekness act when it is mistreated? Jesus said we can learn from Him. How did He act when He was mistreated? He prayed a loving prayer for those who mistreated Him. He forgave them and never stopped loving them, even when they spit in His face. That does not demand that a wife remain hostage in a destructive relationship, but it defines an attitude.

And so, on two mountains, I see meekness in human form. On Sinai, Moses, the meekest person who ever lived, was surrounded by people who did not appreciate either his leadership or his God. When they rebelled against both, God came to Moses and said, "Moses, I want to blot these people out and start over. You can be the hero. You can be the new Abraham. You can be the father of a new nation."

Moses said, "Oh, God, don't do that. If You need to take somebody's name out of the book, take mine, but give them another chance."

Then there is the mountain of Calvary, where they taunted Jesus and ridiculed Him and said, "If you're the Christ, come down." He could have called 10,000 angels, as the song says, to destroy the world and set Him free. But He chose to die alone for you and me. That's like Him, and we want to be like Him.

I'd like to paraphrase this beatitude in these words: "Happy are those in whom Christ lives, for He makes them strong enough to be gentle."

LISTENING TO GOD: THOUGHT QUESTIONS

☞ How do you feel meekness fits into your world? What about your career? Would it be enhanced or hurt if you were more meek?

☞ In this chapter we've described meekness not as weakness, but as strength contained—held in check for God. Does that sound to you like just one more way to work yourself into God's graces, just to grit your teeth and hold it in? What would be the difference between true meekness and just being self-contained?

☞ This chapter describes meekness not just in biblical terms, but in terms of what happens in our own homes. What would happen in your family if you began to display some of the characteristics described here? When are you going to start?

☞ Jesus describes the benefits of meekness in almost heroic terms. These are the kind of people who will inherit the earth. Can you see ways in which demonstrations of a meek attitude could transform circumstances in your world? in your church? in your family?

SHARING WITH GOD: THE MINISTRY OF PRAYER

Lord, I'm no hero, yet I can see how being truly meek would be a heroic act in so many ways, setting in place tremors that would shake my world to its very foundation. Please give me a deeper appreciation for the kind of person You want me to be.

"I pray that You will give me the courage to test Your transforming power. In all candor, I like being the way I am, and that's why I stay that way. But I'm asking You to touch my heart with a vision of what I could be if I allowed You to change me. And I'm giving You permission, just now, to begin the process—whatever the cost.

"Thank You for allowing me to be part of what You are doing in the world.

"Amen."

5 How to Be Happy Though Hungry

Blessed are those who hunger and thirst for righteousness, for they will be filled.
Matt. 5:6, NIV.

*E*arly on a spring morning in 1966 I climbed into a little Cessna 172 airplane and began my first really long cross-country flight as a student pilot. I was headed from southern Michigan to western Canada. I didn't have very many hours of experience, and I didn't have a private license—which meant I couldn't take passengers. But this was an authorized trip, and I would get my expenses paid, and it seemed like a good way to log some hours.

The flight was uneventful across Lake Michigan, Wisconsin, Minnesota, into the Dakotas, and across the border into Canada. Continuing west, I landed in Regina, Saskatchewan, in beautiful country surrounded by rolling wheat fields. I gassed up the plane, stretched my legs a bit, and went inside to check the weather.

Inside I met the pilot of a small commercial plane that was going the other direction. He was also checking the weather, and as we talked I learned that there was a storm ahead.

The other pilot said, "It's a major storm with lots of rain and lots of heavy clouds, but you can probably get over them. I flew over them coming in with no problem at all." So we took off in opposite directions.

I headed west, and it wasn't long before I could see the storm building in the distance. It was about a four-hour flight from Regina to Calgary; there was adequate fuel, about four and a half hours' worth, and I'm not a very good worrier, so I didn't.

Soon, though, I began to see clouds building up between me and the ground. As time went on they got thicker and heavier and more menacing. Then I began to notice that up ahead the storm was pretty high—higher than I thought it would be. So I began to talk on the radio with the weather stations in the area. They said, "Well, you can't go north, because the storm reaches all the way up into the Arctic. And you can't go south far enough to get around it unless you want to go down through New Mexico; it's a gigantic storm front."

I said, "I think I'll just go ahead. I think I can go over it."

They said, "We don't have a report on how high the tops are in your area, but keep in touch."

If you've done any flying in a private plane, you know they navigate by radio. A couple hundred miles ahead there will be a radio station sending out a signal. Pilots tune their radio transmitters to that signal and get the needle to center, and as long as they keep that needle centered they'll fly right to that station. They don't have to be able to see the ground or the station; they just follow that signal. If the needle begins to move to the left, then they turn. If it begins to move to the right, they turn the other way.

They keep that needle centered, and they can fly right to that station from 200 to 300 miles away.

I began to notice that even though I turned the plane a little bit, the needle didn't move. So I began to do a little experimenting. I soon discovered I could turn the plane on almost a 90-degree angle and it wouldn't move the needle at all. The navigation side of my radio had quit. I could still talk to the people on the ground, but now I couldn't see the ground and could not be sure the plane was going in the right direction.

Suddenly I began to get really nervous about the weather. I was two hours out, and I figured I was about halfway. I could see that even though I'd been nursing the plane higher and higher, the storm clouds were still higher up ahead.

I looked at the altimeter: 12,500 feet. Above about 10,000 feet you need oxygen; otherwise you may begin to make dumb decisions. I didn't have oxygen. I thought, *I wonder if I can just go up one more notch to 14,500 and get over them and then go back down on the other side.*

So I began to put a little back pressure on the wheel to get the plane higher. A small plane doesn't like to fly that high. A jet will fly at 40,000 feet, but a propeller plane needs air to pull it through space, and when you start to run out of air the airplane doesn't fly very well. It doesn't do very well at 14,500 feet.

Up ahead the storm loomed higher. So I thought, *Well, I'm out of options for going on. I'd better go back.* And I began to do a little calculating. There were tailwinds at the altitudes at which I had been flying. If I turned around and went back, I would face headwinds. I was halfway; that meant I didn't have enough gas to get back.

Now I was in trouble. In a small plane it's a very dangerous thing to fly through a storm that severe, because some of the churning inside those great cumulus clouds can tear the wings off.

I couldn't go back. I couldn't get around it. I Couldn't go over it. I sure didn't want to go down through it. There weren't many other alternatives. So I did what many young pilots have done—I prayed. And as I looked over the possibilities, the best thing seemed to be to try to pick a friendly place and go down.

So I reasoned, *Well, I know about how high the mountains are here. I know how high I am, so I'll start down through the storm, and I'll watch the altimeter. If I haven't broken out of the bottom of the storm by the time I get within 1,000 feet of where I think the ground level is, I'll pull back up again, fly back out into the clear, and try to find a better place.*

With a great deal of anxiety and with sweat running down my back, I nosed that little plane over and started down through the storm. I set the rate of decent at 1,000 feet per minute, which is a pretty steep descent rate, but I wanted to get down through the clouds as quickly as I could. Suddenly it was as if somebody had painted the windows on the outside. I couldn't see a thing. Rain hammered the windshield.

And all the time this was going on I was praying, "Lord, if You'll get me out of this mess I promise I'll never make such a dumb decision again."

After what seemed to be at least an hour I looked at my watch; one minute had gone by. That meant I'd gone down about 1,000 feet. I could see nothing below. Another minute went by, and another. All the time I was trying to keep the chart on my lap, keep the plane level, keep the airspeed constant, and navigate in what I could only hope was the right direction.

Another minute went by; five minutes. The longest five minutes of my life. Six.

I wondered if anybody was praying for me anywhere. Seven minutes went by. Eight minutes. Now I began to have another concern. How close was I getting to the ground? Was my altimeter exactly right?

Nine minutes went by. I wondered. Ten minutes. I'd gone down 10,000 feet and knew I wasn't very far from the ground. But it was still just as murky and black and raining just as hard as it had been when I nosed into the storm 10 minutes earlier. I looked at my watch and at the altimeter and realized that I didn't have a whole lot of time or altitude to spare. The ground in that area is somewhere between 4,000 and 5,000 feet above sea level.

So I thought, *I'm going to give it another 30 seconds, and if I don't see something by then, I'm going to push the throttle in, climb back up out of the storm, and try to find a different place to crash.*

The seconds ticked by. I was still descending 1,000 feet per minute. Thirty seconds went by. I just couldn't wait any longer. I put my hand on the throttle. I was just ready to push it in when out of the corner of my eye I saw something dark below. I thought, *I'm going to wait another second or two,* and sure enough, there was a little ragged place in the clouds. For a brief instant I could see ground below. What a beautiful sight! I never thought Canada could look so good.

I discovered that I was about 500 feet above the ground, and a few seconds later I broke out of the bottom of the storm. It was still raining so hard I could hardly see forward out of the windshield, but at least I could see out the side windows and know that I was safe, that I was still flying, and that I wasn't going to run into the ground or into a barn.

Looking ahead, I could see off to the side, to the southwest, what looked like a break in the clouds. It looked as if the sky was a little brighter in that direction, so I began to fly toward that daylight. I still wasn't able to do any radio navigation, but I knew that if worst came to worst, I could land in a cow pasture. There is a saying among pilots that any landing you can walk away from is a good one. So I thought, *At least I can put it down in a hay field. It isn't going to look very good on the insurance record, but it's better than something worse.*

With the rain pounding on the windshield, I spotted a railroad track a short distance away. Pilots call a railroad track an iron compass because it usually runs between major cities. So I searched the chart on my lap and discovered a railroad track that ran right into the heart of Calgary, Alberta. I turned and followed that railroad track, and an hour and a half later I was in the approach pattern for Calgary Airport—a very tired but much wiser pilot.

Passion for the Righteousness of Christ

That excruciating hour impressed on me a lesson I will never forget: I was lost, in a storm, and rescue was my only interest.

Have you ever been lost?

I don't mean just temporarily confused, trying to find your way around a strange neighborhood. I mean, *really* lost. There is only one consuming passion for the person who is really lost, and that is to find the way. That's what Jesus is talking about in the beatitude we're studying: "Blessed are those who hunger and thirst for righteousness, for they will be filled."

This is the first beatitude that calls for a passion. "Joyous are those whose lives revolve around a passion for the things of God." Jesus is talking about people who have sanctified tunnel vision. They have one consuming desire in their lives, and that is the righteousness of Christ.

In our affluent age, it's hard for us to appreciate the depth of the meaning Jesus packed into this statement. About the closest most of us come to hunger is how we feel if the oven didn't come on during church—lunch won't be on the table at 12:30.

Even if we're not worried about missing our next meal, who of us hasn't known the pangs that come from being hungry or thirsty? Have you ever taken a long hike and not had anything to drink? Remember how it felt to be really thirsty? A man who is thirsty is not interested in beautiful music. A woman who is really thirsty is not interested in somebody bringing her a bouquet of flowers. They're concerned only about one thing, and that's solving the problem of thirst.

The same thing is true about hunger. Real hunger is not a lukewarm thing. When you've missed a few meals, eating takes on a whole new perspective. Food moves way up the priority list. Jesus knew that well, because just a short time earlier He had experienced real hunger—not just a late dinner, but nearly six weeks of fasting.

Jesus said the truly happy are those who hunger and thirst after righteousness. He said, "I can describe My followers as those who have an unshakable yearning. They have a consuming desire. They long for it, they crave it, they desire it eagerly. They yearn for it, they set their sights on it, they would give their lives for it."

And what is the object of that consuming desire? Jesus said, "They hunger and thirst for righteousness."

Please notice that He did not say, "They hunger and thirst for happiness." Many seek that, you know—running after happiness with the grim determination of a pack of hunting dogs chasing a rabbit. But no matter how fast they run, or how long, or how cleverly, they just can't quite catch it. And the reason is this: Happiness is a by-product of giving our lives to the right cause.

Nobody ever sets out to find happiness and finds it. Can they capture transient pleasure? Probably. Saturday night fling? Perhaps. But not true happiness. Interesting, isn't it? It is possible to get most things you want in life by pursuing them, but not true happiness.

Getting Right With God

What is righteousness? What does it mean to be righteous? What does it feel like? What would it look like? How would we know if we were experiencing it?

At its core, righteousness means to be right with God. It means to have a right standing in His sight, to be in His will. It doesn't mean that I always do the right thing, necessarily, but it means that my relationship with Him is such that even when I've done the wrong thing, my standing is not jeopardized. I can still stand before Him and know that I'm loved and forgiven. Jesus says that the happiest people in the world are those for whom that relationship is the driving passion of their lives.

Then could we say that the truly happy person is the one whose first priority is the daily desire to walk close to God? Is that a good definition? I think so. For example, if that's true, then this beatitude speaks very keenly to our unreserved commitment to a daily quiet time—a daily time we spend getting to know God and coming to understand His will in our choices.

But it's not an easy thing to do. You and I have discovered that. On the contrary, this is where the battle is for the Christian. The real battle in the Christian life is not the battle to overcome sin. It is the daily battle over sanctified priorities—it's about baptizing the Day-Timer.

This beatitude speaks to the solution to that problem. Our "hunger and thirst for righteousness" comes from the time we spend in His presence. This is the only battle we really have to fight: Am I going to walk with Him or not? Am I going to spend time in His transforming presence? Am I going to be with Him?

This insight is to the Christian journey what the multiplication tables are to arithmetic: without it the simplest problems are unsolvable. But we don't need to fight the problems of dress and what we should eat and what we should drink and where we should go and what we should say and how we should relate to our family, because the time we spend in His presence changes those desires and motives and responses that are out of harmony with Him. In fact, this is the only strategy that can change any of these things.

This is the battle the Christian fights. This is where the battle is: time each day spent listening to Him and talking to Him. Nonnegotiable time. But that's so hard! I don't have that kind of time. You don't have that kind of time. When we sit down and look at all that we have to accomplish, where is there time for God?

I struggle with that problem every day of my life. I'm an activist by nature. I'd rather get up in the morning, hit the ground running, and rush to check off the items on my to-do list rather than sit down, open my Bible, and spend the time with Him. It just seems so much more productive if I can get started with my day. There are deadlines to be met, mountains to climb.

But that's so shortsighted. Even to describe it here makes me feel like the man chopping down a tree and not taking time to stop and sharpen his ax. It's like the person who says, "Well, I'd like to tithe and I'd like to give offerings, but I don't have enough money." A person being dishonest with God is never going to have enough. There must be some priorities that set the compass for life. That's what this beatitude is about.

"Blessed are those who take the time that's necessary to maintain that contact, that communion, with Him." This beatitude insists that we ask the question What is the most important thing in my life?

Every once in a while I have to be reminded that spiritually running on empty is not the way of Christian effectiveness. I suppose every one of us has at one time or another made a New Year's resolution about spending some time every day in the Word. We've said, "OK. I'm going to do it. I'm going to start. I'm going to get up early in the morning and I'm going to spend some time." Or "I'm going to block out some time in the evening or just before I go to bed, and I'm going to get into the Word. I'm going to study. I'm going to make it real in my life. I'm serious. It's forever this time."

And the next morning you get up and spend a few minutes reading and praying. The next day you feel good about it. You're really making spiritual progress. You can just feel the spiritual energy surging through your system. But then an emergency arises. There is a late-night appointment and you don't hear the alarm clock the next morning, or you have to go to the office early or one of the children gets sick or the devil creates some emergency—and you miss a day. It's harder to pick it up the next day, and by the third day you're discouraged, and you think, *Phooey on the whole business.*

May I suggest something that's been a help to me? If you have children, you will have an easy time identifying with this. Do you remember when your first baby came home from the hospital? Do you remember the swath that little bundle cut into your schedule? I tell you, when it was time to feed the baby, when it was time for a bath or time for a nap or time for one of the other thousand things babies demand, that baby was in charge.

Do you remember how he or she kept insisting until you answered that call? No matter the hour, day or night? Remember how urgent those cries were? If grandma came to visit, junior still got his bath. If Aunt Nell called up and said, "Let's go shopping today," Susie still got her nap. It didn't matter how short the night had been; when it came time for the morning feeding, the baby got fed. Maybe that kind of attitude toward a daily devotional time might be helpful.

Blessed are those who hunger and thirst after righteousness. That is the description of those who have said, "My time with God, my relationship with God, is the number one priority in my life. Above everything."

Establishing Prayer as a Priority

Ask yourself some questions like these: What are the majority of my waking thoughts about? What subject has my most fervent prayers?

As I asked myself that, I began to do a little mental reflection on what I had been praying about. I discovered that a whole lot of *things* seemed to bob to the top—*things* that we need, *things* I'd like to see happen, other people, schedules, church meetings, balancing the checkbook, getting to the airport on time. I discovered that a lot of those *things* were quite high on my prayer priority list, but seeking God for righteousness was not as far up that list as I wanted it to be. I just needed to hear His invitation, "Be still, and know that I am God" (Ps. 46:10, RSV).

That caused me to do some rethinking of the kind of

things I pray about. Because if I'm going to be the Christian that God wants me to be, if I'm going to carry the imprint of His character on my life, my number one priority must be my time with Him. Thinking that through has changed some of my prayer priorities. When I spend time with God, He doesn't change; I do.

Costa Rica has been the site of a major Adventist World Radio shortwave broadcast facility since 1987. From four medium-size transmitters we broadcast to Central America, parts of South America, and much of the Caribbean in multiple languages. But there are places in the Americas we could not speak to, so in 1997 we began to lay plans to extend our reach. Newer, more powerful transmitters and newer, more efficient antennas. It was logical.

However, as we continued to pray about the project, some of us developed a sense of uneasiness. Maybe this wasn't the most effective strategy. Although we needed to extend our sphere of coverage, we needed to make sure that simply doing more of what we had been doing was the appropriate action.

The Americas are one part of the world in which most governments permit churches and other independent entities to own radio stations. At that time our church owned about 40 such stations, and there was plenty of opportunity for more. But as you can guess, providing good Christian programs for 24 hours every day, or even 18, is a huge challenge, unless you want to play primarily music. But together these 40 stations spoke to more people by far than our shortwave signal did.

So God led us to a rather radical plan. We shut down the shortwave station that had served us well for a decade. We told the management of the 40 stations already operating that if they would send us their best program each day we would edit the programs into a 24-hour block and put them on satellite. We would provide each station with down-link capability, and they could use as much or as little off the satellite as they wished—at no cost to them.

This one gesture changed the face of Adventist broadcasting in the Americas. The stations we were now resourcing had a combined potential audience of more than 30 million—far more than were tuning in to shortwave. We provided the best of programs for these local stations at no cost to them. Anyone who wanted to could start up a station and have instant access to quality programs. At minimal cost we probably quintupled our audience.

I am convinced that those key decisions came about because our leadership team spent the time with God that enabled Him to expand their vision and take advantage of an unprecedented opportunity.

Jesus says in this beatitude, "The happiest people in the world are those whose number one priority is to be in a right relationship with Me." I want that to be my story, and I know you want it to be yours. We don't always get to choose what happens to us in life, but we do get to choose the things we want to aim at—we get to determine our priorities. And if we make a deeper, more vital relationship with God a priority, then God does the hard part.

What Happens When We Do It God's Way?

Fascinating paradox, indeed. "Happy are those who are not satisfied, for they shall be satisfied"?

We've seen Jesus use this technique before in this stirring series of eternal insights. He wants us to allow the Holy Spirit to impress us with transforming spiritual truths. Let me share with you what I think this contrast means. Please notice the emphasis in Jesus' statement: it is not those who find righteousness, but those who seek it, who have the greatest satisfaction. Without being irreverent, I'd like to suggest that it's a little like the Greyhound bus ad: "Getting there is half the fun." Righteousness is not something I ever totally have in my grasp. I can't say, "Wow. Now I've got it. I've had a righteous day." But rather, it's in the quest of becoming like Him that I find the greatest satisfaction.

Keith Miller wrote a wonderful little book several years ago entitled *The Becomers*. That's what we are in Christ: becomers—people who are in the flow of what God is doing in the world, becoming what He wants us to be.

Now, let's be candid. A quest for righteousness looks like dull stuff to the person who isn't deeply searching for God. You talk about the joy in seeking righteousness to the person who is not on the journey, and that individual looks at you as though you're from another planet. But to the person who has discovered the joy in being tight with Jesus, the day-by-day discovery of His will is the stuff of genuine satisfaction.

I'd like to tell you about a quirk of the Greek language. A Greek who said, "I would like some food," used a strange figure of speech. The literal translation would be "I would like some *of food.*" A thirsty Greek would say, "I would like some *of water.*" "I want some water," on the other hand, would mean that that Greek wanted all the water in the world.

But Jesus did not say, "Blessed are those who hunger and thirst after some *of* righteousness." You see, the people He's talking about don't want just "some." They don't want just a little bit. They want the whole thing.

Jesus said, "Blessed are those who set their sights on righteousness." The righteousness, all there is, God's righteousness. And getting there is half the fun. The joy, the excitement, comes in the discovery, in the journey. When I discover something wonderful about God or about His care for me or about the depth of His forgiveness, I think, *Isn't that great?* Then I go back to the Word again and discover there's another meal there I didn't know anything about.

How to Get the Hunger

Maybe you're saying, "I don't really have that longing for spiritual things. I don't really have that desire to be close with God. Maybe sometimes, but not often. What should I do? I am sure it's true that 'happy are those who have the hunger,' but I don't have the hunger. Church is dull. Prayer is boring. I don't like witnessing. I don't enjoy fellowshipping with the saints. I have to force myself to go to church. It's a chore to open the Word."

Are you like that? If you are, don't panic. Don't be discouraged because you think you're so different from those who find a delight in the things of God. Don't fall into Satan's trap of thinking you're a hopeless case—somebody born without the religious gene. You're not all that abnormal. We've all felt that way.

Let me make a suggestion that might prove helpful: Be honest with God about how you feel. He knows you're bored. So be frank with God. Open your heart to Him. He can handle it. Kneel down beside your bed and say, "Dear God, I don't feel like praying. I don't get anything out of it. It's really hard for me to open the Bible. It isn't all that interesting. But I want it to be. I want to have a passion for spiritual things." He loves to answer that kind of prayer.

The story goes that when Jesus fed the 5,000, the little boy who had given up his lunch walked along as the disciples were handing out those pieces of food. He saw that each time a piece was taken, another would come in its place, until they fed that whole multitude. Finally the little boy tugged at the sleeve of one of the disciples and said, "Mister, did you see what that kind Man did with my lunch? Just think what He could do if I would give Him everything."

That's the secret—we can't reach out to God and allow Him to use us without being changed in the process.

Does it happen overnight? Not usually. But what does happen is that the more time we spend with God, listening to Him and being used by Him, the more we come to have our hearts made alive. It starts small and then grows. And then one day we realize we are actually having a great time doing the very things we once thought were dull. The reason is simple: The happiest people in the world are those whose primary focus in life is to walk with God.

LISTENING TO GOD: THOUGHT QUESTIONS

☞ Do you find yourself hungering and thirsting after righteousness? Do spiritual things excite you more than secular things? And if not, what does that say about your spiritual condition?

☞ In this chapter we see Jesus declaring that we need to have a deep and abiding spiritual desire. Do you have role models for this in your church? Are there those who seem on fire for God? What do you think might be different in their lives, compared with yours? Are you that kind of role model? Do you want to be?

☞ This chapter calls for spending time with God each day. In fact, it suggests that activity as the key to spiritual transformation. If it is so central, why is it that so few Christians do it with regularity? Why is it that so few sermons focus on it? How could the church become better at facilitating this? What could you do to change this?

SHARING WITH GOD: THE MINISTRY OF PRAYER

Lord, far too often I don't feel what I wish I did. I'm just going through the motions. I confess that I am often so caught up with the world around me that I feel like a car that is sputtering along, missing and coughing and failing to perform up to Your standard.

"I pray that You will give me a deep, abiding longing for Your presence. I pray that You will lead me into circumstances that test my faith and throw me back on You, making me realize how much I need to spend time with You.

"And even when I don't feel anything at all, I pray that You will give me the persistence to stick with my good spiritual habits, praying, going to church, contributing to Your work, reaching out to help others—because I know that if I do the right stuff, the feelings will follow.

"Thank You for allowing me to be part of what You are doing in the world.

"Amen."

Mercy—There Isn't Much of That Going Around

Blessed are the merciful, for they will be shown mercy. Matt. 5:7, NIV.

For the second week in a row Esther wasn't in church. Mrs. Wallace noticed, and it worried her a little. Esther was a new Christian who had come to Christ from the street, and there were some in the church who weren't sure she was strong enough to survive the tug of old friends and old habits.

Mrs. Wallace had befriended Esther, so she decided to stop by on her way home just to let her know she had been missed. As she walked up the steps to the second-floor condo her worst fears were confirmed. The door was standing open, and there was the unmistakable odor of stale beer. It appeared the others had been right.

Feeling defeated, Mrs. Wallace was about to turn and walk away. She'd call the pastor and report a casualty in God's army. But before she could leave, Esther appeared in the doorway. "Oh, Mrs. Wallace," Esther exclaimed, "thank God you've come. I need you. Please come in!"

Inside, another young woman about Esther's age was standing beside a third, who was slumped forward in her chair at the kitchen table. The third woman obviously had been drinking. The other—well, Mrs. Wallace couldn't quite tell.

During the next few minutes the story spilled out. The night before, the two young friends of Esther's had come to invite her to go bar-hopping with them. Both had been drinking, and Esther wanted no part of it. Instead she was able to coax them inside and began to tell them why her newfound faith made the old life unattractive. One of the young women was interested and wanted to hear more. The other stormed out and slammed the door.

For two hours Esther patiently explained to her friend how her discovery about Jesus had changed her life. As the effect of the alcohol wore off, the effect of the gospel began to sink in. Sometime in the middle of the night her friend surrendered her life to Esther's Lord.

About that time there was a clumsy but insistent knock at the door. Their friend who had stormed out earlier was back. But all was not well. Through her confusion she was able to blurt out that she had overdosed on sleeping pills and who knows what else because she couldn't face what her life had become. The two women knew their best chance to keep her alive was to keep her awake, so now for a dozen hours they had walked the floor with her, sung to her, and rubbed her face with cold cloths.

Mrs. Wallace told me that later in the day, as a degree of normalcy returned to the situation, she found herself asking penitently, "Who was the Christian in this story?"

Mercy Looks for the Best in People

Mercy looks for the best in others. It puts the very best

construction on what it sees. Mercy gives other people the benefit of the doubt. It assumes the best.

The first four of the beatitudes we have looked at are concerned more specifically with inner qualities. But this one, "Blessed are the merciful, for they will be shown mercy" (NIV), speaks directly to relationships—the beneficial effect of the positive use of mercy.

Note the sequence: Christ has not begun to talk about "doing" until He has spent much time on "being." That's what He has been talking about during the first four beatitudes. That's why the Beatitudes are so searching. They tell us, in effect, that as we live day to day we're declaring all the time exactly what we are.

"Blessed are the merciful." What does it mean to be merciful? What does mercy mean to you? I'd like to suggest three ingredients in mercy.

I'm not sure exactly what to call the first one. I know how to describe it, but I don't know exactly how to title it. The word I keep coming back to is "forbearance." Is that a word in your active vocabulary? It's a word from a previous generation and not one we use much anymore. Maybe I can illustrate it better than I can define it.

Do you have a drawer in your kitchen that's kind of a catchall drawer? It's got a partly burned candle, a screwdriver, a bunch of thumbtacks, a roll of different kinds of string, some marbles, and a shoehorn. Nearly every family has a drawer like that. The contents may be a little different, but I'd be willing to bet the drawer is there, holding whatever won't fit anywhere else.

One day a little boy came running into the kitchen looking for a piece of string. He ran over to this special drawer and pulled it out, but he pulled it too far. The drawer came off its tracks and fell, upside down, all over the kitchen floor. String . . . glue . . . candle . . . marbles . . . tacks. His dad and mom were standing there, and his dad really scolded him good. "Awkward! Clumsy! Be careful! Watch what you're doing!" You know the words. Maybe you've even used them yourself.

The little boy forgot whatever the project was and hung his head. He turned and walked out of the kitchen.

A few days later Dad was looking for a screwdriver. He hurried into the kitchen, pulled out the drawer—and pulled it too far. Upside down, all over the floor, stuff everywhere—including under the refrigerator. Mother was standing there watching. Dad stooped down, righted the drawer, and began to put the stuff back in it. He looked up at his wife rather sheepishly and said, "You know, that sure is a short drawer."

Ever since we found that story, whenever a minor crisis arises and somebody in our home thinks one of the others is taking it too seriously, we just say, "Short drawer!"

The short-drawer idea refers to the fact that we can't make everything equally important. Some mistakes are big ones, with far-reaching implications. Others call for a little patience and . . . forbearance. It's a matter of overlooking less-than-catastrophic mistakes, keeping events in perspective.

A driver does something ahead of you in traffic. Someone backs into your new car in the parking lot and doesn't leave a phone number. Somebody at the office lies about you and starts a rumor. You could go off on them, and make it clear that you deserve better and you're not about to be misused. You would have a right to do that, wouldn't you? But do you? Is that the only option available to you? Does the fact that you're a Christian make a difference? Here's an opportunity to practice mercy, one of the ingredients of which is forbearance.

What if one of the big kids down the block punches your little boy, and he comes home crying with blood all over his face? Here's an opportunity to practice forbearance. Or what if a drunk rapes your daughter?

Wait a minute. Now we've moved way out of the area of balls of string rolling across the kitchen floor. Now we're talking about life as it sometimes is. Hard. Mean. Filled with pain and injustice. That's reality. And that's what tests the mettle of a Christian.

"Blessed are the merciful."

Dear Lord, this is so high; how can we attain it? It's so searching; how can we ever measure up? And yet, I look at Jesus as they spike Him to the cross and He says, "Father, forgive them." And I look at Stephen as those stones are slamming into his body, bludgeoning him into unconsciousness, and I hear him say, "Father, lay not this sin to their charge."

And then I discover that we're talking about what it means to be a Christian.

Forbearance is a part of mercy. The beatitudes we have looked at in the previous chapters are basically about attitude. It's possible to play games with those—to put on a front to convince people that we're something we're not. But not here. In this beatitude Jesus is describing how we treat people who are not lovely.

"Blessed are the merciful."

One of the characteristics of the merciful person is forbearance. The humanity in us loves selectively. The Christ in us loves unconditionally. Unconditionally. Long hair and short. With eyebrows pierced or without. Those who agree with us and those who don't. Those who compliment us and those who offend us. Those who are gracious and those who are rude. The neighborhood kid with the noisy motorcycle. The flirtatious woman who makes a pass at your husband. The braggart at the office. The Lord sends us so many of these kinds of people, doesn't He? Have you ever wondered why? Have you ever thought that He might not stop until we learn to love them as He wants us to?

Finding God at Work in People's Lives

The second ingredient of mercy is a word that I hope is a regular part of your Christian vocabulary. It's a word I'm coming to value more and more, although I must admit I still haven't plumbed its depths. The word is "affirmation."

Do you know what it means to "affirm" someone? I don't mean a cheap compliment or shallow flattery. Affirmation means to point out to someone how you see God at work in their lives. Let me illustrate the difference between flattery and affirmation.

Flattery is a compliment I might pay you to try to get something from you. Flattery would be a man going to his boss and saying, "Oh, this is a great place to work. I just love it here. I really appreciate the way you take care of your employees." He is hoping that his attitude will result in a raise.

Flattery is a husband coming home at night and paying his wife a lot of compliments, hoping . . . OK, that's flattery.

Affirmation, on the other hand, is saying, "I see God at work in your life." As we discover that principle in the Gospels, we see Jesus doing it again and again. Look at Matthew 8, just after the close of the Sermon on the Mount. It's so helpful to see how Jesus puts into practice what He's just been teaching.

Notice what Jesus does with this man, beginning in verse 5: "As he entered Capernaum, a centurion came forward to him, beseeching him and saying, 'Lord, my servant is lying paralyzed at home, in terrible distress.' And he said to him, 'I will come and heal him.'

"But the centurion answered him, 'Lord, I am not worthy to have you under my roof; but only say the word, and my servant will be healed. For I am a man under authority, with soldiers under me; and I say to one, "Go," and he goes, and to another, "Come," and he comes, and to my slave, "Do this," and he does it.' When Jesus heard him, he marveled, and said to those who followed him, 'Truly, I say to you, not even in Israel have I found such faith.' . . .

"And to the centurion Jesus said, 'Go; be it done for you as you have believed.' And the servant was healed at that very moment" (RSV).

Notice what Jesus said. They had met just a few moments before. They had exchanged only a few sentences of conversation, but on the basis of the statement the man made, Jesus said to the group of people who were there, "I haven't seen such faith in all of Israel." Now, that's affirmation. Jesus is saying, "God is at work in your life." When Jesus saw that, He pointed it out, not only to the man, but in the hearing of those who stood by.

I don't know about you, but I've been taught that we need to be careful about complimenting people because it might give them a big head. Have you ever heard that? Especially with our children, right? Don't compliment your children—especially in public—because it will go to their heads.

That's a distortion of an important truth. Yes, cheap flattery appeals to pride. But when I say to someone, "I see God at work in your life and it's really a blessing to me," that does not lead to pride. That leads to gratitude. People tend to live up to the reputation we give them. If we constantly tell our children, "You didn't do that well," or "That's just like you," or "Another dumb stunt," they're going to see themselves in that light. But when we convince them that God is at work in their lives, that stretches them, that gives them a divine calling they can live up to; it creates an atmosphere for growth.

This is difficult, sometimes, I know, because what they do is so aggravating and we may feel diminished by their behavior, which reflects back on us. But affirmation steps outside how we feel and allows us to be part of what God wants to do in someone's life.

So the second word I'd like for us to add to our definition of mercy is "affirmation."

One time I was leading a group of young preachers in a classroom exercise. There were about 80 of them divided into groups of six or seven. They had been meeting together every week like this for a couple months. On this day I told them, "Today I would like you to go around your circle and tell each of the others in your group how you see God at work in their lives."

The room was quiet for a long time.

Finally I heard one group begin to talk a little; then another group began to talk. Pretty soon there was general discussion and hubbub all around the room. I let them go on for about 30 minutes, and then we talked about it. One of them said, "You know, Dr. Jacobsen, that was hard work." Another said, "I like the guys in my group, but I couldn't think of anything to say about them." And one of the fellows raised his hand and said, "I think the reason is that we haven't been together very long—only a few weeks."

So we began to look at that a little bit. I said, "You've spent four or five hours in these same little circles getting acquainted, right?"

"Right."

"But in the scripture we studied, Jesus met a man and

within two or three sentences He was ready to say, 'I see God at work in your life.'" Could it be, then, that one of the reasons we don't say it is that we don't see it, and one of the reasons we don't see it is that we haven't been looking for it?

Jesus intentionally looked into the lives of others to see how He could affirm them—so that He could say to them, "I see God at work in your life."

To be freed of the stigma of being judged, and to see, instead, our strengths reflected in the eyes of another caring person, frees us to grow and change. If I'm afraid I'm going to be criticized for what I do, I am afraid to change. But if I know I'm in an atmosphere of acceptance, where even if I do the wrong thing I'm going to be accepted and loved, that creates a safe place from which I can venture into the risky area of changing. That's forbearance. That's affirmation. That's mercy.

The Transforming Power of Respect

The third ingredient of mercy is another key word in a Christian's vocabulary: "respect." Respect for everyone: for the rude; for the woman who backs up in the elevator and steps on your foot and doesn't even say "Excuse me"; for the evangelistic Christian who comes to your door and is insistent about talking to you when the potatoes are boiling over; for the children in your home—and your neighborhood.

We were having dinner at my parents' home in Portland many years ago when our children were small. Somebody handed my dad a dish of garbanzos. The dish slipped out of his hand, hit the edge of the table, and landed upside down right in his lap.

Now, picture this moment: Everybody is dressed in church clothes. We are sitting around the table, being polite and anticipating a nice meal with pleasant conversation.

It's a moment of friendly social interaction. Suddenly the bowl of garbanzos falls into my dad's lap. It's wet and oily and very hot. What do you suppose he does? If your imagination is anything like mine, you can readily envision several rather spectacular reactions.

In truth, my dad did a little vegetarian dance around the dining room for a while. Everyone started scurrying around to clean up the mess. Mom got the dustpan and began to scoop up the garbanzos off the carpet. Someone else got towels and started to mop up the juice. Everyone was waiting for the time when it would be OK to laugh. My dad changed clothes, came back, sat down, and we resumed dinner. It was an incident, but not a crisis.

One of our boys, who at the time was about 8 or 9, said, "Boy, I'm sure glad it was Grandpa and not me who dropped the garbanzos!"

It was a moment of truth. He was right. Grandpa could get by with it; he was an adult. If it had been one of the kids, we probably would have yelled at them. "Look at the mess on the carpet, on the tablecloth, on the suit, on the upholstered seat of the chair! Why can't you be more careful!" Would we have shown the same respect if it had been a 9-year-old who dropped the beans? My guess is that the reaction would have been quite different.

Did you ever read Erma Bombeck's column? Every once in a while she would come up with something that impressed me and that I felt had real heart in it. One piece she wrote about showing respect for your children especially spoke to me:

"I was listening to the radio one day to a child psychologist who said that parents should treat their children with respect as they would treat their best friend—with courtesy, dignity, and diplomacy. I've never treated my children any other way, I told myself. But later that night, I got to thinking about it.

"Suppose our good friends, Fred and Eleanor, came over and I treated them as I sometimes do my children? Dinner might go like this:

'Well, it's about time you two got here! What have you been doing, dawdling? Shut the door, Fred; were you born in a barn?'

'Well, Eleanor, how have you been? I've been meaning to have you folks over for ages.'

'Fred, take it easy on the dip, or it will ruin your dinner.'

'Have you heard from any of the old gang lately? I got a card from the Martins just the other day. They're in Fort Lauderdale again.'

'What's the matter, Fred? You're fidgeting! . . . It's down the hall, the first door on the left, and I don't want to see a towel in the middle of the floor when you're finished, either!'

'How are the children doing?'

'Well, if everybody's hungry, why don't we go in to dinner? You all wash up, and I'll dish up the food. Don't tell me your hands are clean, Eleanor. I saw you playing with the dog.'

'Fred, you sit there, and Eleanor, you sit with the half glass of milk. You know you're all elbows when it comes to milk.'

'Fred, I don't see any cauliflower on your plate. You don't like cauliflower? Have you tried it like I fix it? Well, you try a spoonful. If you don't like it I won't make you finish it, but if you don't try it, forget the dessert!'

'Now, what were we talking about? Oh yes, the Gruebers. They sold their house. I understand they took quite a loss on it.'

'Eleanor, don't talk with food in your mouth; and use your napkin!'

"At that moment in my fantasy, my son walked into the

room. 'How nice of you to come,' I said pleasantly.

'Now what did I do?' he sighed."

Respect. It is a powerful component in mercy.

What's in It for You and Me?

Forbearance, affirmation, respect. An atmosphere of mercy, unconditional acceptance of everyone we meet, respect for the deserving and the undeserving. What a list! The good news is that Jesus lived those traits, and He promises that if we make the journey with Him, He will help us live that way too. And what happens to those who do? Our beatitude says, "Blessed are the merciful, for they will be shown mercy" (NIV).

Do you need mercy? I do.

One of the great self-indulgences seen in the lives of some Christians is the way we are inclined to think of ourselves as the keepers of truth and righteousness—and to forget that we are, at the same time that we minister to others, in utter need of the very things we tell others they need. It's human nature, I suppose, but as we spend more and more time in the church, we tend to reach the place where we see the world divided into two groups—us and them. We're the good guys, and the people who don't know Christ are on the other team. We've got it together, and they're losers.

Now, it's true that God does want us to see ourselves as part of His family and to know that when we join the family we move out from under the death sentence to the promise of eternal life. That's a powerful truth. But no matter how long we've been "in the way," we are no more deserving of God's mercy than we were in the depths of our rebellion.

The pastor needs mercy just as much as the drunk in the gutter. The head elder needs mercy just as much as the pedophile. The Bible teacher needs mercy just as much as the convicted felon. We are never going to reach a point in our lives as Christians where we can say, "Well, I don't need mercy any longer. Now I really deserve being on God's team. As a matter of fact, He's lucky to have me."

The truth is, the closer we come to Jesus, as a result of spending time with Him each day and allowing Him to use us in the great work of compassion and reconciliation He is doing in the world, what really happens is that we come to see our personal need all the more clearly—because we can so much more clearly contrast ourselves with Him. But that recognition of our need doesn't drive us to despair. On the contrary, it fills our hearts with joy, because we realize so much more fully all that God has done for us!

In 2 Corinthians 5:18 we have that remarkable description of what God wants to do with us: "[God] reconciled us to himself through Christ and gave us the ministry of reconciliation" (NIV). We are those who have been given great mercy, and who are then privileged to share the message of mercy with others. We are those who realize that God "has committed to us the message of reconciliation" (verse 19, NIV).

At its core, this is what the good news is all about—God extending mercy to men and women who don't deserve it, and then enlisting them in the process of sharing that incredibly good news with others. And it is what this beatitude is emphasizing: When we are really merciful—in the totally accepting way God wants us to be—our great reward will be a growing realization that His mercy is also directed at us.

Let us then paraphrase this beatitude in these words: "Those who know Christ's forgiveness live joyously as they have the privilege of passing it on to others."

LISTENING TO GOD: THOUGHT QUESTIONS

⌒ The first aspect of mercy discussed in this chapter introduces the word "forbearance," which involves overlooking small mistakes. What, in your opinion, would qualify as forbearance? Are some mistakes too large for us to exercise forbearance?

⌒ In this chapter we also see mercy tied to the concept of affirmation. And we see affirmation defined as sharing with others how we see God working in their lives. How is that different from flattery? What happens when we tell people we see God working in their lives? How would you react if someone shared that sort of thing with you?

⌒ The final insight into mercy in this chapter is that it includes respect. Are there people in your world, such as children, spouse, and people who work for you, who don't get from you the respect they should? How might your relationship change with these significant others if you show them more respect?

⌒ Do you believe that your ability to display mercy toward others may be tied to your own sense of the mercy that's been shown to you? What could make you more able to be merciful?

SHARING WITH GOD: THE MINISTRY OF PRAYER

Lord, I want to be Your person in every way—and I really want to be able to display the sort of mercy that Jesus demonstrated on the cross, forgiving those who were even at that moment causing His death. But I find myself sometimes so filled with resentment over how others have misused me and those close to me that it is like a car horn blaring in my ears.

"I pray that You will give me Your perspective, so that I can

put things in the context You would give them and be able to demonstrate forbearance toward those in my world whose mistakes seem so harmful. I need Your grace for this, because it is too great a challenge for me to face on my own. Teach me to see things from the perspective of eternity.

"And I pray that You will make me into someone who affirms those around me and shows them the kind of respect they deserve as Your children. Take out of me my preoccupation with myself and give me Your love. I need Your mercy, and I pray that You will make me a reconciler.

"Thank You for allowing me to be part of what You are doing in the world.

"Amen."

7 Purity in a Sick World

Blessed are the pure in heart, for they will see God. Matt. 5: 8, NIV.

Kahlid pedaled his bicycle quickly down a dusty path in a Middle Eastern country. He had nearly been caught by the police the night before, and he knew he needed to be more cautious. In fact, this whole sordid life of providing call girls for foreign visitors was becoming more nerve-racking than he had intended. The young girls who provided his living were sweet and pretty and innocent, and he didn't like what he was watching.

As he pedaled, Kahlid was listening to his radio. It had become his only real contact with the outside world. He could keep up with what was happening, even though he was on the run, with that little radio held to his ear.

But this day he heard a different sound. At first there was beautiful music. Then a man with a kind-sounding voice began to talk in his own language about how we are all sinners and how we are all disobedient. Kahlid knew about that from the teachings of his family's religion.

But then, to his surprise, Kahlid began to hear about a man who loved him so much that he had given his life so Kahlid would not have to die for his own transgressions. This was better news than Kahlid knew existed. He stopped his bicycle and leaned it against a low stone wall. Sitting down, he listened to every word. He had never heard such a story. He had never heard the name Jesus.

After a while Kahlid discovered there were tears running down his cheeks. He hurried home and wrote to us at Adventist World Radio. He asked for a Bible and for some kind of help in understanding it. A few weeks later we were able to send a pastor to visit him. Kahlid surrendered his life to this Man who had died for him, and he was baptized. He has now become a teacher in a government school and a force for good in his city. By his own testimony, everything about him has changed since he met Jesus.*

God has promised to do that, you know.

I did a little word study in the dictionary and thesaurus, and I came up with some synonyms for "pure." Here are some of them:

> clean
> transparent
> holy
> innocent
> noble
> always acting from the right motive

Everyone who measures up to that list, please stand up. (Even if I could step outside the pages of this book and look at all my readers gathered in one room, I don't expect I'd see a very large crowd standing.)

"Blessed are the pure in heart." As I read through this list of characteristics that Jesus wants to develop in the citizens of His kingdom, I find excitement on one hand and discouragement on the other. Excitement because of the possibilities—that's what He wants me to be like. And I want to be that way! Then discouragement when I look in the mirror.

A quick survey of Matthew 5—including those beatitudes we've already studied and those we've yet to consider—probably leaves some of us saying, "Wow, these are some kind of spiritual Alps, designed for the Christian mountain climbers among us—those hearty souls who somehow leave us mere mortals behind and go on to greater heights." Our attitude is that just a select few can ever make it. The rest of us plod back and forth on the misty lowlands—admiring those who do it all, but knowing it's just not in our futures. Have you ever had the feeling that God's expectations are so high you can never reach them, so tall that you can never possibly measure up? Have you ever thought, *That's what I'd like to experience—but it's always just out of reach?*

There are times in every Christian's journey when we feel we're making progress. We can look back and see how far we've come. Maybe the mountains we've climbed are just foothills, but at least we can see that we've conquered. We've all known the exhilaration of a habit overcome or a temptation resisted. But even when we have this experience, we know there in the distance are those great mountains of spiritual success, and we fear we'll never set foot on them. If you have felt that way, please remember this one fundamental perspective: the beatitudes are not goals God asks us to achieve. Rather, they are promises that He wants to fulfill in us.

"Blessed are the pure in heart, for they will see God," Jesus says to us. Notice: He does not say, "Be like this and then you'll get to see Me." Many of the religions in the world say that. "Get your act together, and you will be rewarded by arriving at the place where God is." It's the sort of thing the human spirit expects religion to suggest.

Jesus, in vivid contrast, says, "This is what I want to do in you. Do you want to go along for the ride?"

Christlikeness, that's our goal. We strive for it. We study to achieve it. We pray for it. We plead for it. We go to church, hoping to come closer to it. We go to camp meeting, searching for it. And all along it is God Himself who is prepared to give it to us. What a profound revelation!

The High Standard of Jesus

In this beatitude Jesus holds up before us another one of those high standards. "Blessed are the pure in heart." Who among us has not wished for absolute purity in our thought life? Who has not wished for absolute integrity in submitting an expense report? Who has not wished for purity of heart at income tax time? God has placed in our hearts a desire to experience this.

On the other hand, what student has not sat down for a final exam and wished they had some outside resources to be of help, even if it was their neighbor's paper? Who has not faced the reality of temptation?

I received a letter a few years ago from a man who had been a seminary student in one of my classes, now a young pastor. It read:

"Dear Dr. Jacobsen,

"I'm in my first district now. My wife and I are really enjoying it here. We're so glad to be out of school and be out in the work at last.

"The reason for my letter, though, is to tell you something that I have had on my heart for a long time. You remember a book that you asked us to read in a certain class? I handed in a report saying I had read the book, but I had not. And now, as I'm here trying to live a Christian life in front of the people in my community and my church, I need to get that off my conscience. I need to make it right. Please write and tell me what I should do.

"Sincerely,"

I responded to the young man and told him how much I appreciated his writing, how it brightened my day to see a man who wanted to have his life right with God, even if it involved the embarrassment of writing a letter of confession. I commended him for his sensitive spirit in wanting to make everything right. I suggested that he go ahead and read the book, because it would be an inspiration in his ministry. He wouldn't have flunked the course even if he had admitted not reading it at the time, so I didn't have to go back and change the gradebook.

Are there things in your life that you wish you could go back and change? Are there things you wish you'd had the strength to resist? Absolute integrity. Uncompromising honesty. Pristine purity in every thought. Motives always beyond reproach. Now, those are the Alps of Christian behavior. Who of us lives at that altitude?

And our generation, better than any before us, has honed the skill of making the obscene appear attractive. It's almost embarrassing to page through *Newsweek*, to go to the bookstore, to stop in front of a magazine stand, because almost anything you see is being marketed on the basis of the appeal to the sensuous and the impure. As a Christian is bombarded with a constant diet of the lewd, it is obvious that it's going to take supernatural resources to live as Christ wants us to live.

And yet the desire to be pure in heart continues to resonate in the Christian heart. We long for it. We know how fulfilling it would be to have nothing lying between us and God.

I've been asking the Lord to help me know how to share with you the reality about what Jesus would like to do in our lives. And how He would like to do it today. I'd like to share with you some of the most exciting things I've ever discovered as a Christian. I believe that the Lord is going to allow us to put our fingers on some resources that will be a life-changing help as we let Him do within us what He wants to do.

How God Designs to Change Us

Here is what has happened to us—the biblical explanation of the crisis we all face: "The god of this age has blinded the minds of unbelievers, so that they cannot see the light of the gospel of the glory of Christ" (2 Cor. 4:4, NIV). And here is God's solution: "Do not conform any longer to the pattern of this world, but be transformed by the renewing of your mind" (Rom. 12:2, NIV).

Do you see the inevitability of this answer? It is only through our minds that God can communicate with us. Our minds are the basic distinction between us and the rest of the animal creation. A monkey has a stomach. A cow has a heart. A dog has ears. But only people have rational minds that can conceptualize God and can communicate with Him.

I found a beautiful statement in the book of Psalms some time ago. I'm sure I had read it before—many times probably—but somehow it had never grabbed my attention as it did this time when I was studying, seeking to discover how God wants to do His purifying work in my heart.

Psalm 107 (NIV) begins with a long detailed list of the miseries of God's people, Israel. Phrases such as, "Some sat in darkness and the deepest gloom," "They stumbled, and there was no one to help," and "They loathed all food and drew near the gates of death." It is a frightful litany of their history. But in verse 20 is this dramatic statement describing God's antidote: "He sent forth his word and healed them."

"He sent his word and healed them!" What an insightful phrase! There is a transforming power in the Word of God. He sends His Word to heal us, to undo the damage that has been done by sin. God says that transforming power, healing power, is inherent in His Word.

Let's explore exactly how that works.

The Bible is the Holy Spirit's book. Men and women whom God chose spoke as they were directed by the Holy Spirit. As we take His Word and explore it and digest it and memorize it, the same Holy Spirit who oversaw the writing of the Book gains access to our minds. For instance: the fruits of the Spirit are love, joy, peace, patience, kindness, goodness, faithfulness, gentleness, and self-control. Fruit doesn't grow on its own. It grows because it is attached to the vine.

Here is what happens: God says, "Take My Word into your life every day. Spend some time with that Word regularly. And as you do, the Holy Spirit comes in, bringing with Him His fruits. As those fruits begin to flourish, they displace those traits of character that are un-Christlike. Love replaces lust. Joy, peace, and kindness replace guilt, fear, bitterness, and selfishness.

From the Psalms again: "How can a young man keep his way pure? By living according to your word. . . . I have hidden your word in my heart that I might not sin against you" (Ps. 119:9-11, NIV). David had it figured out.

There is no other way to live purely in a sick world. The struggle includes too much that's against us, and the influences we are battling are too cunning. There is a supernatural battle going on here, and we can be victors only with supernatural strength. God has promised, "I'll change you from inside. I'll heal you through My Word."

There's a book I have come to appreciate because of my background as a teacher. It's entitled *Counsels to Parents and Teachers,* by Ellen G. White, and on one page of that book are three of the most amazing statements I have ever read. If all the other literature in the world were suddenly destroyed in a nuclear blast and this one page came fluttering down to earth, we'd have all the incentive we need to study the Word.

Please read these profound sentences carefully: "If the mind is set to the task of studying the Bible, the understanding will strengthen and the reasoning faculties will improve. Under the study of the Scriptures the mind expands and becomes more evenly balanced than if occupied in obtaining information from books that have no connection with the Bible" *(Counsels to Parents and Teachers,* p. 452).

And in the same book, on the same page: "He who gives the Scriptures close, prayerful attention will gain clear comprehension and sound judgment, as if in turning to God he had reached a higher plane of intelligence" *(Ibid.).*

God said, "I sent my word to heal them."

And once more: "He who makes these truths a part of his life becomes in every sense a new creature. He is not given new mental powers, but the darkness that through ignorance and sin has clouded the understanding is removed" *(Ibid.).*

That's how it works. How does God's Word heal? It's not a magical power. It's not a mystical power. As we study it, the darkness that ignorance and sin have caused to the human race and to your mind and mine is banished—and

...at is the healing God promises.

It may not be dramatic. It probably won't be overnight. But it's like putting money in the bank. You put a little bit aside every payday, just a few dollars. It doesn't seem like much. It doesn't seem very sensational. But later on a need develops, and we discover there are resources to draw on.

The same thing happens with our regular exposure to God's Word. It may not seem dramatic. We may go away thinking, *Well, no bells rang this morning. I didn't hear any sirens. No whistles.* But we put a little bit more away, and then when it comes time to draw on that account there is something there.

The beatitudes are not about a destination; they are really about a journey.

Locking the Words of God in Your Heart

Do you memorize scripture regularly? Every time I bring up this topic, someone says, "You know, I'd like to, but I'm too old." Or "I haven't memorized anything since I was in school. It's all I can do to remember my own phone number."

Let's work on that. There are three secrets to memorizing. One is interest. The second is frequency. And the third is familiarity.

Now I'd like to do a little experiment. Psalm 117 is a very interesting passage of Scripture. Matthew's Gospel says that after the foot washing and the Communion service, "when they had sung a hymn, they went out to the Mount of Olives" (Matt. 26:30, NIV). Scholars tell us that Psalm 117 is the hymn they sang.

Think of the significance of this psalm to Jesus. Here He was, facing betrayal by His closest friends and an excruciating death, carrying the sins of the world on His heart, yet

He led His disciples in singing this psalm of praise. That background gives us good motivation to become familiar with this short scripture, and even strong incentive to memorize it.

But let me tell you something else about it: It's Hebrew poetry. Hebrew poetry does not rhyme; it's in parallel verse. In other words, the poet will make a statement and then say the same thing using other words. Watch for that as you read.

"Praise the Lord, all you nations; [then he repeats the same idea]

extol him, all you peoples.

For great is his love toward us, [then He repeats]

and the faithfulness of the Lord endures forever.

[Then the little refrain at the end]

Praise the Lord!" (NIV).

There are really just two lines, which are repeated, and then the refrain, "Praise the Lord." Would you take a minute right now and read the psalm out loud? Go ahead; try it.

Now let's commit it to memory. Read it again. Remember the structure, just two lines, each repeated in other words, then the refrain at the end. Read it from the page above. Now see if you can quote it without looking. How did you do? Good. Once more. Again. Well done.

Let me encourage you by saying that you memorized an entire chapter of the Bible in just a couple minutes. That's the entire 117th psalm, both verses. So, you see, you can memorize scripture.

But you might be saying, "I've forgotten it already. It's already slipped my mind." That may be, but, you see, repetition is the secret. Write it out. Put it on a card. Tape it above the sink in the kitchen. Put it on the bathroom mirror. Tape it to the steering wheel. Put it under the glass on your desk, or in your shirt pocket so that when you're waiting at the stoplight or you've got a few minutes, you can work on it.

When you're jogging in the morning, stick it in the pocket of your sweats. Repeat it as you jog. As it becomes part of your memory it will become part of your mental processes and you'll never forget it.

I had that reinforced in my mind very dramatically when I studied Morse code. Randy, our younger son, was serving as a student missionary in Bolivia. He wanted me to learn the Morse code so we could talk on ham radio. I said, "Randy, I'm sorry. I just cannot learn that stuff."

But he urged me, "Dad, try it."

As I tried to learn the dits and the dahs and how to communicate in Morse code, I would turn my ham radio on and listen to a series of dots and dashes and I would think, *How in the world can anybody keep up with that stuff?*

But it came. I spent a few minutes in the morning and a few minutes in the evening listening to those code tapes. I finally memorized the letters, and my speed began to build. It wasn't long before I was able to communicate in Morse code.

At first I thought it was a physical impossibility. But by repetition, a few minutes in the morning and a few minutes at night, I committed the Morse code to memory. I should have suspected that, because the same thing is true with almost anything we want to memorize.

Remember the three secrets of memorization? Interest. Familiarity. Frequency. It works with the Word.

Walking in the Presence of God

When Jesus refers to the pure in heart, His comment about them is that "they will see God." They will walk in His presence. But that's not all. The idea that the pure in heart will see God is also a promise of an eternal reward.

The promise that we will "see God" is the promise that the relationship we have with Him here will continue into eternity. What a promise!

Then a closing paraphrase might be: "Happy are those who regularly spend time with God's Word, for they discover that He changes them completely, from the inside."

LISTENING TO GOD: THOUGHT QUESTIONS

☞ A major thesis of this chapter is that the Beatitudes are not goals God asks us to achieve, but promises that He wants to fulfill in us. How does that make you feel? Is it liberating? Does it give you hope?

☞ Another major insight in this chapter is that we can't change our behavior until our minds have changed, through an inner renewing that comes from regular exposure to God's Word. What is it about God's Word that could cause such a profound effect on us? What parts of Scripture should we focus on, and why?

☞ An appeal is made in this chapter to begin memorizing scripture. Are you planning on taking that appeal seriously? Here is something very direct and practical that you can do to change your life. It's not vague. It's not theoretical. Spend time in God's Word, and you'll be changed. Why not start today?

SHARING WITH GOD: THE MINISTRY OF PRAYER

Lord, I'm constantly embarrassed over what I see in the world around me. It's as if I'm being bombarded by impurity and ugliness everywhere I turn. I feel as if I'm being shaped and molded into that way of thinking—often without my conscious choice. I know there is no way I can stand against all that in my own strength.

"I pray that You will give me the faith to turn to You and Your Word—daily, systematically—so that the power of good so profoundly displayed in the life and words of Jesus, and in the rest of the Bible as well, can crowd out the evil that wants to dominate my mind.

"And I pray that You will give me the clear mind and steadfast purpose to resist the temptation to fall back into old habits and get so busy that I slip away from spending time in the Word. I understand how vital Your Word is in helping me stay close to You, and I commit to You my best energies.

"Thank You for allowing me to be part of what You are doing in the world.

"Amen."

---

*The details of this story have been changed to protect Kahlid.

Licensed to Get Into Trouble

Blessed are the peacemakers, for they will be called children of God. Matt. 5:9, NRSV.

Being a Christian means getting into trouble.

Now, there's a radical thought! We're not supposed to stir up the trouble intentionally. We're not to go about looking for people to irritate. But when you and I became Christians we were licensed to get into trouble. Being a Christian—in the context of God's call to a radical new way of living that we're exploring in this book—implies a willingness to wade in where there is trouble and be a peacemaker, an intercessor, a reconciler, a bridge builder. Paul says that God's people are ministers of reconciliation. We talked about that briefly in an earlier chapter. Now we're facing it square on as a very explicit call from God.

The definition of "reconcile" I like best is "to cause to be friendly again." Isn't that a great description of what needs to be going on in our world? We're to be the people who step into difficult situations and cause people to be friendly again.

Jesus said it even more simply in Matthew 5:9: "Blessed are the peacemakers, for they will be called children of God" (NRSV).

We said as we began this book that the Beatitudes are Christ's radical charter for a new way to live. This beatitude is a good illustration of why we've used the word "radical." As Jesus neared the end of the list, I suspect that the disciples and the others who heard Him were staggered by the dramatic picture of the new kind of life He was calling them to live. We get accustomed to it because we read it so often; the words become familiar and they do not jar us. But for those who heard them for the first time it must have been staggering.

Jesus said to His disciples, "You will never again be satisfied with the safe, cautious, self-seeking, tame, isolated existence you have known. You cannot hide in your cloister." He said, "You cannot take refuge in your fishing boat anymore. You cannot hide in the hills and be a hermit. You cannot sit any longer in your tax-gatherer's booth with complacency. I have stood you at attention, aimed you at the center of the world's need, and said, 'Forward, march!'" I can almost hear the marching music!

A Ministry of Reconciliation

Let's make sure this one thing is clear: Jesus does not expect us all to make great fortunes in this life. He does not expect us all to make a great name for ourselves. He does not expect us all to make a great splash in history or a great earth-shattering discovery. But He does expect us all to make peace. He expects us to enlist in this ministry of reconciliation.

As is the case with other of the beatitudes we've looked at, there is a dissonance here. It immediately raises the question Why does it say we're to be peacemakers, and yet, just a few chapters later, Jesus says, "Do not suppose that I have come to bring peace to the earth. I did not come to bring peace, but a sword" (Matt. 10:34, NIV)? How can He, in chapter 5, commend His disciples for being peacemakers, yet say in chapter 10, "I didn't come to bring peace"? How do you make those two images fit?

I'd like to suggest that Jesus came to bring a sword to those things that ought not be together, and to bring peace and reconciliation to those things which ought not to be apart. Jesus came to drive a sword between truth and error. But He came to bring peace between husbands and wives. Jesus came to bring a sword between integrity and compromise. But He came to bring peace between the generations. Jesus came to drive a sword between love and lust, because they are so different. But He came to bring peace among all races. Jesus came to drive a sword between sin and righteousness. But He came to bring peace between the human family and God.

To read through the Bible story is to be absolutely convinced that peace is a high-priority item in God's scheme of things. It is mentioned more than 400 times in the Bible. Jesus is called many things, but near the top of the list He is called the Prince of peace. Peacemaking must have a high priority in God's will for His people for Him to give His Son that name.

Let's talk about the need for peace, first of all, in our homes. Would you describe your home as a peaceful place? Maybe we ought to define it by contrast. We're talking about peace, not just about truce.

Look at the history of our world and the way the nations have so seldom been at peace with each other. Someone has said that peace is simply the brief lull when everybody stops to reload. That kind of peace exists in some homes, too—just the little interval when people stop to reload. That's why someone has said that most of what goes under the guise of listening in family arguments is really only standing in line to talk.

Presenting the Elijah Message

In the last chapter of the last book of the Old Testament is a most fascinating prophecy, the final one before the New Testament story begins. "Behold, I will send you Elijah the prophet before the great and terrible day of the Lord comes" (Mal. 4:5, RSV).

You probably know about the "Elijah message." Elijah came to the land of Israel at a time of great compromise and rebellion. God gave Elijah a message to proclaim that was to bring men and women back to the worship of the true God, in the right way, on the right day. Elijah was God's instrument of dramatic reform. See 1 Kings 18 and 19.

But the prophecy in Malachi 4 is that a similar message of reform will be heralded across the world before Christ comes the second time, and that one of the results of that message will be to bring families together. "He will turn the hearts of fathers to their children and the hearts of the children to their fathers" (verse 6, RSV).

I am blessed to know that our families are that important to God. I'm so thankful for the renewed emphasis on families I am seeing in the church all around the world. Men and women are saying, "I believe God wants to change me. My prayer is not 'Dear Lord, change my obstreperous husband,' or 'Dear Lord, please help my son to quit what he's doing and behave himself,' but rather 'Dear Lord, help me to be the kind of person You want me to be so You can use me to be helpful in the lives of my family.'" The Elijah message does that. The message that we are to herald in the last days changes families.

Have you ever come to a place in your relationship with your children where you've said, "I just don't understand my kids?" Let me share a couple secrets: They don't understand you, either. You didn't understand yourself when you were that age, and they don't understand themselves. But you don't have to understand someone to love them.

Several years ago I clipped a Dear Abby column out of the newspaper. It began with a letter from one of her young readers. "Dear Abby," it said, "my dad doesn't understand me. My dad thinks I'm . . ." And the writer went on to describe the breach between himself and his dad, the lack of understanding, how his dad did not understand the things he did.

Then the son concluded his letter by saying, "But there is something else I need to include in this letter, and that is that I don't understand why I do some of the things that I do either. Neither has my father ever stopped loving me, even when he didn't understand me."

The Elijah message preached in the last days is not simply to create a body of truth we can take home and put on the shelf and say, "Isn't this wonderful? I have the truth now! Look everyone, here's the truth . . . over there by the fireplace." Rather, if the Elijah message does its work in my heart, it's going to make a difference in my home. And there will be more forgiveness going on in the Christian home than anywhere else in the world. That's His promise. As that message does its work it brings the generations together. Maybe there have been some walls that have grown up, things you just didn't understand or things you wish your children had done differently. Or maybe it was a spouse who has embarrassed you—or betrayed you. The gospel reaches across the chasm those events have built, and hugs.

Several years ago in a large church in the Midwest, the youth department was invited to come and lead out in the program for morning worship. The main part of the program was four young people who were to present the gospel in music. They made several mistakes, one of which was to bring a bass guitar. Bass guitars really make some folks nervous. The young people themselves had written the songs they sang, one or two of which stretched the coping skills of that conservative congregation, as you might imagine. But one of the songs was over the edge for some of the members. The title was "There's a Devil in the Land," and it described rather vividly some of his activities in our world. The further they went into the song, the more uncomfortable some of the folks in the congregation became.

Finally one man got up and stormed down the aisle and out the back door. Outside he accosted the pastor. "If you're any kind of spiritual leader, you'll go in there, stop that program, put those kids in their place, and apologize to the church."

If you had been the pastor, what would you have done?

Well, the program concluded, and the saints filed out. It was evident from an inventory of faces that a lot of strong emotions—both pro and con—had been generated during the preceding hour. Too many to ignore.

The pastor discovered that this group of young people met every Thursday evening to practice in a hall a couple miles from the church. So the next Thursday evening he and his wife went to the building where they were rehearsing. They slipped in the back where it was dark, sat down, and listened.

For perhaps 10 or 15 minutes the young people didn't

know they were there, but then someone spotted them. The pastor and his wife slowly walked to the front and sat down on the floor by the piano. The kids knew why they had come. And so, after they had sung a little more, a conversation began. About music. About good taste. About a sense of the appropriate. About forgiveness. And understanding.

Their argument was: "The songs were theologically correct, and it's the music that expresses the experience we're having. People ought to be able to accept that." The pastor tried to help them see that if nobody is following, you're not leading. For an hour the young people, the pastor, and his wife talked together.

Several good things came out of that discussion, and the best is that those young people are still loyal and effective Christians today. If the pastor had yielded to the pressure and denounced them from the pulpit, I'm not sure that would have been the case. I believe that was peacemaking between the generations—what God wishes us to do.

More Than Mere Tolerance: A Call to Building Firm Bridges

Let's talk about another aspect of being peacemakers. I can think of no more dramatic way in which sin distorts the human experience than when one person looks with disdain on another for no other reason than the color of the skin. That certainly must say something about the way sin has corrupted the human heart. It must be because we have lost an appreciation of the fatherhood of God that we have lost the sense of family in His world.

I'm not just talking about peaceful coexistence here. I am not describing condescending toleration. I am not asking that we simply refrain from contributing to the war. Peace is not just cessation of hostilities. Nowhere is Jesus called the Prince of truce. He has not called us to be peace-keepers but peace*makers,* and that is the title of one who wades intentionally into the tensions of the world to build firm, lasting bridges.

The issue of race isn't something we can stand back and let take its course. Every born-again Christian will be an advocate for reconciliation between diverse ethnic and racial groups.

I want to tell you about Frank. He was a member of a medium-size church on the East Coast. One day a Black family began attending and applied for membership. It was a first for Frank's church. The Black family already held membership in his denomination, but not in this local con-gregation. A short time later Frank decided he would join the choir. During a break in a rehearsal Frank discovered there were strong feelings in the choir about the new family, so strong that the choir voted to disband if they were granted membership. As Frank listened to the arguments, he found himself beginning to agree and soon was a leader in that cause. He said, "If we let them in, it will start a trend. We don't want any of 'them' in here with 'us.'"

Frank's son, who was 6 at the time, asked his daddy why the choir had disbanded. When Frank began to hedge in answering his son's question, his guilt level began to rise. The contradiction of the gospel that it presented began to stir in his mind. As a result of his son's simple question, Frank had a change of heart.

Frank went on the initiative again. He went to the home of every choir member, confessed the part he had played, and asked their forgiveness. He prayed in every one of those homes. He pleaded, interceded, began to reeducate, and finally brought reconciliation.

His attitude, his peacemaking, brought new acceptance

within the choir, and out of it came a new understanding of Christianity to that entire congregation. If you visit there today you'll find one of the finest little choirs in the East. And standing side by side, singing praises to the God of all the human family, are Frank and his new friend—from that Black family.

"Blessed are the peacemakers, for they will be called children of God" (NRSV).

Bringing People Into Peace With God

There's one more aspect of peacemaking I want to talk about: Whoever leads someone else to renounce sin and yield their lives to Christ is a peacemaker. That's really the task to which God has called His church.

Once when we were moving from a home in which we had been living, a neighbor said, "You folks have sure fixed up your house nicely." We had tried to take a real interest in the yard. We had done some landscaping and a lot of fertilizing, mowing, and planting. Without solicitation one of our teenage sons piped up and said, "Yeah, they've never moved out of a house that they didn't leave better than they found it."

I liked that. It was a nice compliment—particularly from one of my own children. I was glad he could observe that. But it caused me to do some heart searching. Ruthie and I got to talking about it later and I said, "I wonder if we've never moved out of a *neighborhood* we didn't leave better than we found it." That's a harder question, isn't it? If you were to move out of your neighborhood now, would you leave that neighborhood a better place than you found it? I wonder if that's true of my neighbors. If I were to move out of my neighborhood now, would I leave my neighbors better people than they were? Would they have been blessed because we had lived among them?

I believe it's time for Christians to make some bold decisions about the kind of people we're going to be, and for us to take some bold actions relating to how we're going to become involved in Christ's radical charter for a new way to live.

A little boy knocked on author Ann Kiemel's* door one day. As she tells the story:

He was dirty and hot and he had wads of newspapers under his arm.

"Would you like to buy a paper, lady?"

"Well, what kind of paper is it?"

"Grit."

"Grit? What kind of paper is that? I never heard of it."

"Well, ma'am it's a paper I'm selling and it talks about . . ."

Well, I couldn't have cared less, but I looked at him and he looked so tired and worn out so I said, "Okay, how much?"

"Quarter."

So I went and got a quarter. "What's your name?"

"Buster."

"Hi, Buster. My name is Ann. Doesn't it get pretty hot walking these streets every day?"

"Yeah."

"Pretty tired?"

"Yeah."

"Buster, I'd like to be your friend. And whenever you're out selling papers, if you get real thirsty or real tired, I want you to know you can come to my place, and I'll give you some cold Kool-Aid and let you sit down in the cool and we'll laugh together. How does that sound to you?"

"Pretty good."

LICENSED TO GET INTO TROUBLE

And so Buster started stopping by my house. I guess just because somebody cared about him. And he needed someone to care. One day I said, "Buster, take me to your house. I'd like to meet your family."

He sort of shuffled his feet. . . . "It's not a very nice place and I don't think you'd like it."

"Buster, I don't care where you live. I just want to go with you."

He took me to a little shack with two rooms, a bathroom and one big room, and a father of some 80 years of age. Buster, his little sister and his father all lived there. Their alcoholic mother had deserted them years before and only dropped in now and then. . . . I had never been in a place like that in my life. But I was out to love Buster to Jesus. He was part of my world and I really cared for him.

One day Buster said to me, "Do you like fishing?"

"Well, I guess so. I mean I'm not a very good fisherman. I hardly ever go fishing."

"Would you go fishing with me sometime?"

"Sure, I'll go fishing with you. Where do you go?"

"Well, there's a pretty good drain ditch up the road."

"Oh, when did you have in mind?"

"How about Saturday morning?"

"Saturday morning?" I had only one day to sleep in and that was Saturday morning. But, after all, if you love someone you have to make sacrifices.

"What time, Buster?"

"What do you say about 5:30?"

"Buster, I know the fish wouldn't bite at 5:30. That's way too early."

"Yes. That's the very best time—5:30 in the morning. That's when they really bite."

"Are you kidding me, Buster? Fish actually bite at 5:30

in the morning?"

"Sure they do."

"Well, okay love. Come by at 5:30 and we'll go to the drain ditch."

If we were going to a big lake it would have been more exciting. But a drain ditch—at 5:30 in the morning?

He knocked on my door 15 minutes early and I wasn't out of bed yet. I jumped into some old clothes and we headed for the drain ditch. He had dug a can of fat slimy worms.

When we got there I said, "Buster, I tell you what. I'll hold the worms while you fish 'cause I really don't know a lot about fishing. . . . Maybe later we'll switch."

So I seated myself on a cold, hard rock, holding the can of worms and Buster went down to the ditch. It was in his heart. He wanted me to see him catch a fish. He was determined—and he tried. . . .

"Buster, I told you it was too early."

"Shh. Be very quiet."

So I'd sit there looking at those ugly worms, praying, "God, please help him to catch a fish so we can hurry and go."

After a while, the sky began to get darker and darker and soon it began to pour.

"Buster, are you sure fish bite in the rain?"

"Sure, they bite anytime."

"Even in the rain, Buster?"

"Yeah, it's no problem."

And the water began to run in my hair. I was getting desperate. "God, will you please hurry up?"

Buster was not leaving without a fish. Finally he caught one. And we were both dirty and wet and we got in the car. Now with a fish in the can of worms.

On the way home, I said, "Buster, are you hungry?"

"Yeah."

"Would you like to stop at a coffee shop and get something to eat?"

"Wow! You mean a restaurant?" . . . He thought he'd like that.

It just so happened that there must have been fifty businessmen having breakfast on Saturday morning. Well dressed, sophisticated. And we were dirty and smelled like fish. And they seated us and I whispered, "Now, Buster you can have anything you like. If you want five eggs and three pieces of bacon then you order it."

So he did. . . . Five eggs and bacon. And when the waitress walked away he whispered, "Ann, I never been in a place like this. This must be the best in town!". . .

I loved Buster.

Everytime the social worker would come to his house his father would send Buster on his bicycle to me. "Go get Ann. I need her down here quick."

I made all the family decisions. I decided what they did with their money. I prayed them through the rough times. I told the father what to do in every situation. He began to lean on me as if I were his eldest child. I baked fudge and cookies. I'd laugh with Buster. I'd walk with him. Buster and I cried together.

Buster would tell me how embarrassed he was of his house. And every time I dropped him off my heart ached.

Did Buster come to Sunday School? Only about three times in two years.

But you see, I was out to love Buster. Not if he came to Sunday School. Not if he did what I thought he should. Just to love him. Through thick and thin. To love him even after I got him a new suit and he overslept and didn't make it to church—to love him anyway.

Buster's in the service now but I hear from him. He's

about to get married. "Ann, there's only one person in my life who ever really loved me. And God lives in me because you loved me." Just a simple little thing like loving him brought God into the life of ordinary Buster.

A lot of times you tell people God is love. And they laugh. "Are you kidding me? Do you see where I live? Did you see my Dad beat me last night? God is love? I don't buy it." The only love people in your world will understand is you. God and you loving them. Then they'll believe.

"Blessed are the peacemakers, for they will be called children of God" (NRSV).

LISTENING TO GOD: THOUGHT QUESTIONS

✍ We live in a world that seems to thrive on conflict. As you interact with that world, what should your priorities be? What is the relationship between being right and being a peacemaker? What should you do when those two seem in conflict?

✍ Who should take the initiative in helping to create reconciliation within the family? The parents? The children? Paid counselors? Can we ever expect to understand people of another generation? Do we need to in order to be peacemakers?

✍ What could you do to make your church a more intentionally diverse family of believers? What should you do when you hear others make statements or take actions that serve to keep the races at odds with one another? Is there a difference between tolerating differences and becoming an agent for reconciliation?

SHARING WITH GOD: THE MINISTRY OF PRAYER

Lord, I know my own heart. I know that dark ugly impulses rise up in me when my views are challenged or my assumed rights are threatened or discounted. Too often I'd rather win myself than see everybody win. And that makes me part of the problem, not part of the solution.

"I pray that You will give me no peace until I'm able to become a peacemaker. Don't let me settle for standing on the edges, out of the fray—believing that it's OK to be a spectator. Give me the courage to step into the middle of things and serve as Your minister of reconciliation, whatever the cost.

"And I pray that You will give me a passion for making this happen in my own family. Help me to share Your love so powerfully that these people closest to me sense that I've been with You, and want the same experience for themselves. Help me love them for You in the way You love them Yourself.

"Thank You for allowing me to be part of what You are doing in the world.

"Amen."

---

*Taken from *I'm Out to Change My World* by Ann Kiemel. Copyright © 1974 by Impact Books. All rights reserved.

9

Smiling Through the Tears

Blessed are those who are persecuted because of righteousness, for theirs is the kingdom of heaven. Blessed are you when people insult you, persecute you and falsely say all kinds of evil against you because of me. Rejoice and be glad, because great is your reward in heaven, for in the same way they persecuted the prophets who were before you. Matt. 5:10-12.

*T*here are few areas of the Christian life that stir up more confusion than the question of persecution. Should we expect it? Do we need it? When will it start? Why would God allow it? What does it mean if we're *not* being persecuted?

I'd like to give you five true-false questions to ponder as we introduce this theme:

1. There is persecution of the Christian church in North America today. T/F

2. We ought to pray for persecution, because it will purify the church. T/F

3. If we were really living godly lives, there would be more persecution. T/F

4. If a Christian is being persecuted, it

is because he or she is living a holy life. T/F

5. Persecution develops holiness. T/F

Let's try to come to some common understanding on the answers—even though we probably can't expect unanimity.

Is there persecution of the Christian church in North America today? At the risk of sounding paranoid, I think our answer to that question would have to be Yes, there is some. Yes, if you consider the political pressures directed toward many in public office, for instance. Do you remember when President-elect George W. Bush chose Senator John Ashcroft to serve as Attorney General in his new cabinet? It immediately created a storm of protest, not just regarding Ashcroft's previous political and legislative positions but because many were afraid his Christian perspective somehow disqualified him for high public office. (Now there's one that would bring a perplexed frown to the faces of the founding fathers!)

Who can forget Columbine High School and the chilling story of Cassie Bernall? Two deranged fellow students brandishing rifles asked her if she was a Christian. She looked them full in the face and answered, "Yes." She died where she fell.

Not all religious persecution is that dramatic. There are families in which it's tough to live your faith. There are workplaces in which you're the object of mockery if you won't exchange lewd stories around the water cooler. There are campuses on which, if you thank God for your lunch in the cafeteria, you may end up with mustard in your hair.

When we move beyond the shores of North America the presence of opposition to Christianity escalates dramatically. Fifty percent of the population of the world live in countries where the spread of the Christian faith is forbidden or restricted. Many of the hundred thousand letters in more than 50 languages that we receive every year from AWR listeners tell of the precarious conditions under which they must practice their new faith, often because of government restriction. Much of the mail we send to listeners who write to us at one of our Adventist World Radio studios we send back in handwritten, personal-looking envelopes, because we don't want to get our listeners in trouble with the authorities who are antagonistic to Christians.

Is the Christian church undergoing persecution today? Probably more than we know.

2. Should we pray for persecution because it purifies the church? This one undoubtedly deserves a No. It's an interesting experience to hear someone pray for God to bring on persecution. Have you ever heard it? It goes like this: "Lord, bring down persecution, because the church needs it so we can be shaken out of our lethargy." And you always feel as if the person is about to add "And please start with someone else."

Probably we would agree that many of us need to awaken from our self-satisfied sleep. But it is not God's plan that we depend on persecution to accomplish this. The winds of persecution can't blow embers into flame unless the embers are hot. True spiritual vitality comes from a relationship with Jesus. It doesn't come from some external force pounding us.

It is, rather, a simple fact that genuine holiness often brings persecution. The sequence is an important one. Get the sequence wrong, and you're walking down a very dangerous path.

3. If we were really living godly lives, would there be

more persecution? This one gets a Maybe. Or perhaps a Probably. We'll consider this more fully further into our discussion of this beatitude, but let me suggest that as Jesus grew up He "increased in wisdom and in stature, and in favor with God and man" (Luke 2:52, RSV).

While it's true that all who live godly lives in Christ Jesus can expect to suffer persecution (2 Tim 3:12), it doesn't mean it will happen to everybody all the time—as is demonstrated by the life of Christ. He was persecuted and put to death. But He didn't endure persecution all of His life.

Persecution will come. We don't need to go out looking for it or feel guilty when it hasn't yet arrived.

4. If a Christian is being persecuted, is it because he or she is living a holy life? Not necessarily. It may be because he is being a real stinker and is bringing it on himself. She may be presenting her faith in such an aggressive, offensive manner, so filled with self-righteousness and condescension, that onlookers respond by saying, "If that's what Christianity is like, I want no part of it."

Persecution comes in many forms. Some of it is because the person being persecuted stands out of the crowd in a righteous sense—serving as a true witness for God. Sometimes it comes because the people doing the persecuting are dark and ugly on the inside.

5. Does persecution always develop holiness? No. It can also develop cowardice. How we react to persecution is based on the quality of our relationship with Christ. It drives us either into the arms of Christ or into hiding.

The fact is, persecution typically reveals what is inside us more than it changes us. Those who know Jesus respond to persecution in an entirely different way from those who don't. And if you're not now on a committed spiritual journey, spending time getting to know Jesus, don't expect the onset of persecution to make you into somebody you're not.

Reflect with me on a composite of the person we've been describing throughout this book. Jesus described these people as humble, sorry for their sins, under the Holy Spirit's control, longing to be more like Him, looking for ways to be helpful, transparent in their dealings with others, making peace wherever they go. What would you say about people who live like that? Pretty nice to be around, wouldn't you think?

Imagine that someone introduced a stranger to you and said, "Here is what my friend is like: humble, penitent, spirit-filled, Christlike, helpful, honest, and peacemaking." What would you say? "May I have your autograph?" But in reality Jesus warns us that this ladder of spiritual development doesn't lead to praise and accolades. It very often leads to opposition and persecution. He says, "You're developing characters like this? You can expect hostility and hatred for your trouble."

It's a great paradox.

The Paradox of Persecution

But why? Why is persecution the natural result of living this kind of life?

In our world spiritual vitality often provokes opposition and hatred because holiness is a disturbing element. People are irritated when you give a disapproving glance at their story of deliberate dishonesty—some cute little thing they did with their taxes or an expense report. It agitates them when you choose to ignore a suggestive comment they make about an office secretary. It bothers them when you don't let your son go with theirs to a creepy-crawly movie. It irritates them when you're the only one at the office party who has a Fresca. It frustrates them when you won't take part in a strident labor dispute in which they're involved. It perplexes them to know that you can give away 20 percent of your income, close your business on the best business day of the week, pay to send your children to a private school, and still drive a respectable car.

It makes them envious that your children don't come in at night drunk like theirs. It embarrasses them that they have a smoker's cough and you don't. Your tranquillity in the face of tragedy perplexes them. Jesus says, "You wish to live as I lived? Then you can expect to be treated as I was treated. Not always. Not by everybody. But you can expect it."

When Jesus demonstrated those qualities of holiness that set Him apart from the world in which He lived, they tried to kill Him.

This beatitude contains a warning, though. I need to be sure that it's the Holy Spirit who is making my friend uncomfortable around me and not my obnoxious attitude. This is no promise of happiness for those who are persecuted for being crotchety or cantankerous, those who exercise poor judgment, or those who are abrasive to their neighbors.

"Blessed are those who are persecuted because of righteousness" (NIV).

I was in South Vietnam during the Vietnam War, near the city of Da Nang, visiting with one of our Adventist GIs. We had been chatting for an hour or so when he told me that he was being given a hard time by his commanding officer. He said, "He really doesn't like the fact that I'm a Christian, and I have a hard time getting my Sabbaths free. He gives me more KP than anyone else, and I'm really being picked on because I'm a Christian."

So I said, "Mel, I'll go talk to him and see if we can't get it worked out."

I made an appointment with his commanding officer. But I soon discovered that the man was not being persecuted because he was a Christian. He was being disciplined because he was lazy. The officer gave me some times and places, and he said, "This fellow is just plain lazy, and the reason I give him more work is for punishment. If he's telling you that it's religious persecution, he still hasn't gotten the message."

Jesus never promised happiness to those who are persecuted because they are lazy or crotchety or hard to get along with or because they have an abrasive personality or because they are always talking when they should be listening. Remember: "Blessed are those who are persecuted because of righteousness" (NIV).

Persecution and the Church

It is seldom the compromising who are persecuted for righteousness' sake. It is not a lukewarm church that draws persecution. In our world, vital holiness provokes opposition and hatred because holiness is a disturbing element.

Holiness is a disturbing concept to those who are not intent on pursuing it. One of the reasons hard feelings can develop within the church is that there are many Christian people who do not like to have the ease with which they live in sin disturbed. And someone else in the church whose life is obviously committed to Christ and to holiness can be a thorn in the side of a person who doesn't want to get too close to Christ for fear it will be confining. The person who is living a lukewarm, arm's-length Christian experience can feel very uncomfortable in the presence of a person whose life is genuinely and deeply committed to Jesus Christ.

That's what made Jesus so unwelcome in various settings during His ministry. Logic would say that they'd have liked to have Him around—just on general principles. What an asset He could have been in time of war. If there were battle casualties, He could have healed them. If the troops ran out of food, He could have provided it. If the navy was about to be swamped by a vicious storm, He could have stilled it. But His holiness disturbed them. They knew they weren't like that, and it made them uncomfortable. In fact, so vicious was their hatred of holiness that they finally had to dispose of it.

Whenever we talk about persecution I suppose there's a temptation to become morose and morbid. There's a time of persecution coming to God's people. Scripture is clear on that. What shall we do? How shall we endure it? It is altogether possible that many who read these pages will one day pay a high price for their faith. But Jesus says, "When you're talking about being persecuted for your faith, don't become morose and morbid, but rejoice." Rejoice? How can that be? How can we think about persecution and rejoice?

I think the apostle Paul has the best counsel for us in Scripture, because he certainly knew what it meant to be persecuted for his faith.

"Rejoice in the Lord always. I will say it again: Rejoice! Let your gentleness be evident to all. The Lord is near. Do not be anxious about anything, but in everything, by prayer and petition, with thanksgiving, present your requests to God. And the peace of God, which transcends all understanding, will guard your hearts and your minds in Christ Jesus" (Phil. 4:4, NIV).

This is no armchair general who is counseling us. This is no spectator in the cheap seats, yelling instructions to the coach. Paul wrote that from prison. It is in the midst of that persecution that he could say, "Rejoice when you're persecuted." When the kids at school make fun of you, you can love them in return. The ultimate act of courage is to love the people who do you wrong. Jesus showed us how.

Let me suggest three reasons that we can rejoice in the face of persecution: First, it is often through persecution that the cause of truth is advanced. I remember reading a statement when I was in college that impressed me enough that I have remembered it for a half century. It said, "The blood of the martyrs is the seed of the church." History documents that claim. So when you and I are called on to suffer for what we believe, it can be an instrument in the hand of God to see the truth go forward. God means that truth shall be brought to the front and become the object of examination and discussion even through the contempt placed upon it. And if there is a worthwhile reason for what we're enduring, it gives us the strength to hold on.

The second reason we can rejoice in persecution is that it often gives us an opportunity for a personal witness. Here's the apostle Paul, chained to two soldiers, preaching to them. I'm confident those two soldiers who were chained to Paul's wrists got a full dose of the gospel during their duty hours every day. Here was an opportunity for Paul to do some witnessing to a different group. He wasn't standing in front of a church, but he was still preaching the gospel.

So when there is persecution in the air, what should we do? Look around and see just who it is God wants us to meet. He may have set up a meeting for us, and we don't want to miss it.

And third, when God's people are persecuted for living

the kind of righteous lives that bring Him honor, we can rejoice that the holy character for which we've been hungering and thirsting is being seen in our lives. That can be a strong personal affirmation. If others in the office are aware that when they tell an off-color story you're not going to laugh, that's one of the ways that you can know that God is, indeed, doing His work in your life.

No wonder God can counsel us to rejoice in the face of persecution for righteousness' sake; issues are being surfaced. We have an opportunity for a personal witness, and it's a strong affirmation that God is doing His work within.

I would not for a moment make light of the reality of persecution. The fact that the hand of God can be seen in it does not mean it's fun. Read through that Hebrews 11 catalog of God's saints. It says that some were torn asunder by wild animals, some were sawn in two, others starved to death or died of thirst. And yet there can come a deep inner joy because we know that the persecution is part of the price we're paying for the holy lives God is developing within us.

Victory Through Persecution

Back to the Matthew 5 passage where we began. I'd like you to notice something Jesus does here. As I studied this beatitude I discovered it is the only one in which Jesus really expands His basic theme. The others are very short, only a few words, but this covers three full verses. Verse 10 begins, "Blessed are those who . . ." That's the way He's been talking in all the others. But then in verse 11 He turns as if to look them in the eye and says, "Blessed are you when men revile you and persecute you and utter all kinds of evil against you falsely on my account" (RSV).

There is no promise of rescue from persecution for

God's people. Christianity is no fire escape, and there's nothing that says that because you're a Christian you may be taunted but you will never be tortured. In fact, millions have been tortured for their faith in Christ. Jesus says, "I want you to go into this with your eyes open. Don't be fooled. This is a sinful world. You're in enemy territory. If you don't believe Me, check the record. Millions have died for their faith."

Jesus says, "Remember, persecution does not change the basic attitude of Christians. They'll still rejoice, still maintain their spirit of meekness, of humility, of forgiveness, still display their desire to bring peace. To be able to stand in the midst of a group of persecutors who have spit in your face and say to them "I still love you" is to know something of the deep need each of us has for the spirit of Christ within that brings holiness. It is not a human characteristic. It is a supernatural characteristic that comes into the life only as Jesus lives there.

Then He says, "Spend time with Me and I'll give you the power to do that." What an honor!

Jesus says, "Rejoice and be glad, for your reward is great in heaven, for so men persecuted the prophets who were before you" (RSV). What a great list to be on: Moses, Amos, John the Baptist—and Don Jacobsen. I like that. He is putting us in a great company of those who were persecuted but emerged victorious. What a concept!

Final Words

Well, there we are, standing in the crowd, listening to Jesus give His inaugural address. The sun is hot, and people all around us are discussing what He has said. We've just heard Him outline a call to a radical new way of living. He hasn't pulled any punches. We know what we're in for if we choose to join up with Him. There will be good times and bad—and a lot of the time we'll be out on a limb, just trusting Him. People we love may come to hate us. We could well be placed in circumstances that will test our faith and courage. Some of us will perhaps even die for our faith. But what a high calling He has given us that we can join Him in His noble redemptive work for Planet Earth.

You look at the man standing next to you in the crowd. "Well, what do you think?" you ask. "Quite a preacher, isn't He?"

"I don't know," he replies, shaking his head sadly. "I thought He was going to rally the crowd to go after the Romans. I thought He would tell us what we could do to throw them out of the country. I guess I'm disappointed. I didn't understand most of what He said. It was so . . . religious, you know?"

"He was telling us that it's not the Romans we need to worry about," you reply. "The changes need to be in us, in our hearts and in the way we treat one another. It's a whole new way of looking at the world." It all seems to make so much sense to you. In fact, you're feeling a wave of something akin to excitement that is invigorating your spirit. To be partnered with God in this great work!

"But I came here to see if He was the one who could lead us to overthrow our enemies. That's what I want," the man says.

"Don't you see that He's offering us something far better?"

The man gives you a strange look, as though you've lost your mind, and wanders off into the crowd. The fact is, not everyone is going to find what they're looking for in the words of Jesus. Even some who sit next to us in the pews of the church. The appeal Jesus is making in the Beatitudes is an invitation for us to let Him do the deep work within us that He wishes to do. He's asking us to step outside the traditional way of looking at the world and looking at people and embrace a new reality. He's asking us to accept a whole new ethic, a new appreciation of what He is doing in the world and how we can be part of it.

Some who sit in the crowd listening to His words are going to choose to remain in their familiar comfort zone. They're going to hold back, acting as though they don't grasp the radical nature of what Jesus is doing, when it's really that they just don't want to change. "Why can't things remain as they are?" they ask. "Church is such a comfortable place."

But what Jesus is telling us is that we can't hide. We're either part of the solution or part of the problem. Events are racing to their inevitable conclusion, and we can be part of what God is doing, or we can become an obstacle to it. We can stand up, or we can be swept away with the crowd. There really isn't any other choice.

"Rejoice and be glad," He says to us. We can be on the winning team. On Jesus' team. He's making a call for a radical new way of thinking and living. Are you going to embrace it? The choice is yours. The choice is mine. How are you going to choose? I know my choice. Join me, won't you?

A few weeks after the shooting at Columbine High School, Cassie Bernall's mother wrote, "I am able, ultimately, to see the loss of my daughter not so much a defeat as a victory. The pain is no less. It will always remain deep and raw. Even so, I know that her death was not a waste, but a triumph of honesty and courage. To me, Cassie's life says that it is better to die for what you believe, than to live a lie."

LISTENING TO GOD: THOUGHT QUESTIONS

☞ Not all of us are experiencing persecution today. Should we be doing something to bring it on? Should we be doing something to deserve it? How should you look at persecution?

☞ How would we know if the persecution we do experience is the result of sincere efforts at holiness—which means God is bringing it on—or merely because of our offensive personality? How do we draw the line between standing for what's right and appearing as self-righteous prudes?

☞ A major focus in this chapter is how we can rejoice when we're persecuted. Is that something that makes any sense at all to you? Why would someone who's in pain rejoice? Can you list some good results that can come from being persecuted? Are you ready for this experience? Are you spending time with God so He can make you ready?

Final Question:

☞ This entire book has been about Jesus' call to a radical new life. It's about not settling for business-as-usual Christian living. Is that something you want in your life? Are you ready for Him to lead you down the paths that test you and transform you and ultimately position you to be His person for this time?

SHARING WITH GOD: THE MINISTRY OF PRAYER

Lord, thank You for allowing me to see a little more clearly what You want to do in my life—and in the life of the church and the world. I know there is much more You want to show me, so I pray first for spiritual perception.

"Then I pray that You will give me the courage each day to stand up and say, 'Yes, Lord, I'm Yours to do with as You choose. Mold me, shape me. Use me in the ways You want.'

"*Finally, Lord, I pray that You will give me a passion for the things of God. Help me to love people the way You love them. Help me to love the truth as You love it. Help me to want to change the world the way You do.*

"*Thank You for allowing me to be part of what You are doing in the world. Set the path, Lord, and help me follow it.*

"*Amen.*"